NATURAL SCIENCE OF THE ANCIENT HINDUS

ICPR SERIES IN NATURAL AND SOCIAL SCIENCES

General Editor: D.P. CHATTOPADHYAYA

Towards a Critique of Cultural Reason
R. SUNDARA RAJAN
(New Delhi: Oxford University Press 1987)

Essays in Social and Political Philosophy
Edited by KRISHNA ROY and CHHANDA GUPTA
(New Delhi: Allied Publishers Limited 1989)

The Primacy of the Political
R. SUNDARA RAJAN
(New Delhi: Oxford University Press 1991)

SURENDRANATH DASGUPTA

NATURAL SCIENCE OF THE ANCIENT HINDUS

EDITED BY
DEBIPRASAD CHATTOPADHYAYA

INDIAN COUNCIL
OF PHILOSOPHICAL RESEARCH
New Delhi
in association with
MOTILAL BANARSIDASS
Delhi Varanasi Patna Bangalore Madras

First Published 1987
Reprinted 1991

Published by Member Secretary for

INDIAN COUNCIL OF PHILOSOPHICAL RESEARCH

Rajendra Bhavan (Fourth Floor)
210 Deen Dayal Upadhyaya Marg, New Delhi 110002

in association with

MOTILAL BANARSIDASS

Bungalow Road, Jawahar Nagar, Delhi 110 007

Branches

Chowk, Varanasi 221 001
Ashok Rajpath, Patna 800 004
16 St. Mark's Road Bangalore 560 001
120 Royapettah High Road, Mylapore, Madras 600 004

ISBN: 81-208-0329-9

PRINTED IN INDIA
BY JAINENDRA PRAKASH JAIN AT SHRI JAINENDRA PRESS, A-45 NARAINA INDUSTRIAL AREA, PHASE I, NEW DELHI 110 028.

General Editor's Note

Philosophy of Natural and Social Sciences has been of scholarly interest for a long time both in India, Europe and in the Semitic world. Of late, this interest has both deepened and broadened. Many philosophers maintain that philosophical categories and concepts are somewhat empty and speculative unless they could be meaningfully related to the studied conclusions of natural and social sciences. Some even go to the extent of affirming that philosophy itself is a social science. There are other philosophers who think that unless natural and social sciences reflect on their own presuppositions, methods and aims, their fuller implications would not be revealed. It is primarily keeping these views in mind that ICPR Series in Philosophy of Natural and Social Sciences is being introduced to philosophers, social and natural scientists, and the general readers as well.

The publication of *Natural Science of the Ancient Hindus* by the late Professor Surendranath Dasgupta has been made possible mainly because of the kindness of Dr (Mrs) Surama Dasgupta, the wife of the author of this book and who herself is a distinguished scholar. ICPR is deeply grateful to her for giving it the manuscript of the book which she has preserved with scholarly care.

ICPR is also grateful to Dr Debiprasad Chattopadhyaya, well known for his works on the History of Science and Technology in India, for kindly undertaking the responsibility of editing this difficult manuscript left behind by Professor Dasgupta.

New Delhi
March 1987

D.P. CHATTOPADHYAYA

Author's Preface

It was with some degree of hesitation that I had to choose the title of this book. I do not know if I have done it rightly, but I had no other alternative since nothing better occurred to me.

I have not collected here some of the empirical facts which were known to the ancient Hindus but I have tried to put in a condensed form the main features of the conflicting theories of matter, motion and cosmic changes held at different times by different schools of philosophy—Hindu, Buddhist and Jaina. I have purposely omitted many interesting empirical facts which some other writers had mentioned before. I have noted only those facts which are necessary for illustrating the theories. Many of these are here brought out for the first time. I have tried to demonstrate that the views the Indians held on matter, motion, etc. were not the results of mere guesses but were consistent deductions from definite systems of philosophy and often the result of a close and systematic chain of reasoning. How far these ideas can be compared with ancient and current ones on similar subjects in the Western world, it is for the readers to judge.

The book consists of two independent papers written at different times and for different purposes. There could thus be no integral connection or unity of purpose behind them as could be expected from a work written under one single idea with one purpose in view. It will not be out of place to mention briefly the circumstances under which these were written.

Sometime in 1915, Sir Devaprasad Sarvadhikari, then the Vice-Chancellor of Calcutta University, asked me to supply him with some information about the notions of the Evolution Theory of the Hindus, which, I was told, some Professor from America had enquired of him. After six month's work I wrote a paper which I then called *Pariṇāma and Evolution*. I read out the paper to him at his residence and left it with him as he wished to send it to America. Subsequently my esteemed friend Sir John Woodroff borrowed the paper from him and utilised it in his *Śakti and Śākta*, where he was kind enough to acknowledge it.

I do not know the name of the American Professor for whom

Sir Devaprasad had wanted it; he himself forgot the name and could not remember it when after some time I had asked him.

In 1917, Sir J.C. Bose and Sir Rabindranath Tagore requested me to read a paper at the Summer Meeting of Darjeeling. I had then with me a copy of this *Pariṇāma and Evolution*. But it appeared to me that the work could be read in such a meeting only if it could be substantially changed by the addition of some new matter to give it a new shape. I worked upon it for some days and read the paper with the illustrious Sir J.C. Bose in the Chair. Sir J.C. Bose found that it contained many interesting facts about the knowledge that the ancient Hindus possessed and he was rather agreeably surprised. He requested me to leave the paper with him, but as it contained many technical facts he found it rather difficult to follow, asked me to send him a synopsis of the main facts expressing the wish to write an article on it in *Nature*. At his request I prepared a synopsis of my paper but I do not know if he wrote any article in *Nature* about it.

I tried to publish the paper later in some of the leading journals of India; but there was no philosophical journal in India at the time and it was found too philosophical or technical for journals of general interest.

In January last Sir Asutosh Mookerjee, the greatest patron of learning in living memory, had an opportunity of seeing my paper. He was kind enough to take a very lively interest in it and requested me to hand it over to him for publication. I found that my paper *Evolution Theories of Ancient India* (as I called it at the time of reading it at the Darjeeling Summer Meeting) could be materially improved if I could make further additions to it. But the time at my disposal was very limited as I was then on the eve of departure to England and so I could not add all that I wanted to. I could add another paper to it, *Matter and Motion*. I changed the name of the original paper *Evolution Theories of the Hindus* into *The Theories of Cosmic Changes*. I am very glad that Sir Asutosh Mookerjee had of his own accord wanted to publish it from the Calcutta University. If fortune allows it to pass through a second edition I hope to find ample opportunities of making considerable additions to it, which I cannot do now for want of time.

Contents

Editor's Note v

Author's Preface vii

Part One: MATTER AND MOTION 1

Part Two: THEORIES OF COSMIC CHANGES 51

Appendix: Genesis of Tanmātras 85

Notes 91

Index 95

PART ONE

Matter and Motion

The progress that Europe has made in the domain of Natural Philosophy, commonly called Science, in its various branches, during the last two centuries is incomparably greater than what it made during the twenty preceding centuries. Philosophy also has witnessed wonderful developments in modern times beginning from Descartes; but it seems clear that philosophy could never so captivate the minds of the people as science did. The genius of the Western nations has probably found its truest, sincerest and most successful expression in the development of science and its handmaid, mathematics. Other nations of the world are also trying to acquire this scientific temper with some success, but still they are to be regarded more or less as apprentices.

This development in Europe and America has been so great and varied that even when studied merely from the theoretic point of view, each subject (e.g. physics), presents a number of branches every one of which requires lifelong study and research. The benefits conferred by the cultivation of science have been such that people now have much more material advantages, comforts and objects of enjoyment than what they could even dream of before. The whole social environment has been so changed, the old barriers and limitations in the way of human intercourse have been so removed and all the economic, social, intellectual and physical forces of the diverse nations have been so brought together, that it has altogether changed the phases of future human prospect.

It cannot however be definitely asserted that this has increased the sum total of human happiness, but it seems that Europe has at least up till now found in it the best expression and realisation of the inner cravings of its soul. Neither philosophy nor religion, but science and science alone is the *summum bonum* of Europe. Without yet being very categorical, it seems to us that the attitude of looking at the comforts of life as the principal object of all our endeavours underlies all the scientific hankerings of the present age, and this was probably so even in the old Hellenic times. Plato and Aristotle are not probably the true representatives of the Greek life; they are rather examples of individual philosophical geniuses. Greek life was more easy-going, practical and comfort-seeking than what we are led to think about it by reading Plato and Aristotle. This Hellenic spirit had for a long time remained in abeyance during the dark ages of medieval times, but as soon as the shackles and chains which had bound down the minds of men in the old dark corner were broken, Hellenism began to reassert itself with the Renaissance in varying forms of desires for control over nature and the consequent advancement of material advantages aimed at and brought about by all scientific developments. Renaissance had not probably brought forth any element which is absolutely new, but has probably revived in a new form and shape the old Greek temper of mind.

India, however, produced from the earliest times, in a long series of succession, great thinkers who had risen far above the superstitions and lack of reason of the common masses. But such was the speciality of Indian temperament that it always found its longings and cravings, as manifesting themselves in an yearning after the Infinite, realisable only in philosophy and religion. People indeed took to the different useful arts and industries. But the discovery of the laws of nature and the ways in which such discoveries may be made useful for the service of man were not what they enquired most. Stray speculations are no doubt found here and there but these always have lesser interest, and are brought in only as subsidiaries to the philosophical craving of the Indian mind. The man in the street knows neither philosophy nor religion but still, even now, he would unhesitatingly say that philosophy as leading to the highest realisation of mankind was more necessary for the happiness of men than the control over nature of which Europe is basically proud. Religion and philosophy are the things in which India has expressed itself entirely and most satisfactorily. Ideas with regard to the construction of the internal world find expressions in most systems of Indian philosophy, but only with reference to its place in a constructive scheme about the ultimate truth involving the microcosm and the macrocosm.

There is practically no indication in the whole field of Indian literature that any investigation regarding the laws of nature or the chemical properties of matter merely for their own sake was pursued, except what we find in Hindu astronomy and medicine. In Hindu medicine, instructions are found with regard to the formation of many metallic compounds. If any treatise of Hindu chemistry is possible, it will only mean the enumeration of certain elements and compounds that the Hindus knew and prepared for medicinal purposes. Dr. P.C. Ray has written on Hindu chemistry, but it is disappointing in the sense that it does not deal with chemistry in the present European sense of the term: it only treats of certain compounds and their preparations and nothing more. But this is an inevitable difficulty, for this is all that can be found about chemistry. Similarly, it will not be possible for any one to write a work on Hindu physics in the modern sense of the term, but one can collect passages from different works to demonstrate the theories of matter and motion of the Hindus. These theories are never worked out in detail but only find expression in connection with philosophical and other ideas which formed the main topic of the writer. At the same time it is interesting to see that these ideas often reveal the keen analytic and imaginative powers of the Hindus, who in the course of such stray thoughts were sometimes led to the very problems about the ultimate constitution of matter with which the most gifted physicists of the day are busy. As I have already said, the Hindus never busied themselves about the investigation of the laws of nature except in so far as it was connected with the general philosophical speculations.

To begin with, the idea of matter or mass that the Hindus had, the earliest passage that comes to my mind is the one given in the great grammatical commentary of Patañjali (150 B.C.). According to it, the suffixes *tva* and *tal* are attached to words to denote qualities (*guṇas*). The qualities are those sensible properties such as sound, touch, colour, taste and smell; that which is different from all these is called a thing (*dravya*). Is the *dravya* (thing) different from the qualities such as sound, touch, etc. or identical with them? The fact that the existence of certain qualities in a thing leads to its being given a name shows that the thing is different from its qualities. But it may also be said that the thing is not different from the properties of sound, touch, etc., for nothing else than the qualities (*guṇa*) are perceived. We may divide an animal into hundred parts, putting them on hundred leaves, but in none of these parts do we find anything else than the said sensible properties. But even then it has to be admitted that a thing is different from its qualities, for though we may not perceive the thing yet its existence may be known by inference, just as though we do not perceive trees and plants to grow or decay yet their growth or decay may be known to us by inference or, just as the movement of the heavenly bodies may be known to us by inference; so it is here too.

What is the nature of this inference? Though the length and breadth of a lump of iron and cotton be the same, yet when they are placed on the scale pans of a balance one side goes down and the other goes up. There must be some cause for which this happens. That cause which creates this difference between iron and cotton is called *dravya* or a thing. Again there are things which break at a mere touch and there are others which do not break even when they are stretched forth. That which causes this difference is called a *dravya* or thing. Again there are some which may be split in one stroke whereas there are others which may not be split even in two strokes; that which causes this difference is *dravya* or thing. Rather, a thing is that the essence of which is not changed in spite of the change of its qualities. If asked 'What is this essence?', we say that it is the being of the thing. A plum or an *āmalaka* fruit is sometimes yellow and sometimes red; but it is all the while a plum or an *āmalaka* and the identity is never changed with the acquisition of new qualities. A *dravya* is so called because the qualities assemble (from the root *dru*, 'to flow to') in it.[1]

In another place while distinguishing between a class notion and an individual thing, Patañjali says that even an individual material object such as a cow or a horse including all the sensible properties that it possesses is *dravya* (thing).[2]

The word *dravya* was thus used by him in two senses. First in the ordinary sense of matter or material thing, the individual objects of our visual perception as just referred to.

Secondly in the sense of mass forming the essence of matter as has been referred to in our first quotation from *Mahābhāṣya*.

The conception of mass is indeed a difficult thing, but we find that Patañjali has been able to express his idea through the help of varying illustrations fairly well. Mass or *dravya,* according to Patañjali, is that which gives a thing its relative weight: it is that which is also regarded as the basis of the greater or lesser cohesiveness of the atoms constituting a thing. It is regarded as the permanent basis of matter which is the receptacle of all changes of qualities. Patañjali thinks that the sensible properties of a material thing do not give us the whole truth about it; but there are other data from which we may infer that in the background of these qualities there is *dravya* or the mass, as the underlying principle of all material things which is that seat of the qualities—sensible or otherwise. Apart from these sensible qualities there are other phenomena connected with material things which cannot be accounted for without the supposition of the existence of mass or *dravya.* These phenomena, as Patañjali notices, are those of relative weight (as indicated by the sinking and the rising of the scale-pans), the greater or lesser cohesive connection of the atoms or probably greater or lesser density. He also describes it as that which conveys to us the sense of persistence amidst all changes of qualities. In explaining the purport of Patañjali's idea of matter, Bhartṛhari says in his *Vākyapadīya* that it is regarded as different from the individual objects and it is called by various names such as *ātman* (soul), *vastu* (thing) *svabhāva* (nature), *tattva* (reality) and *dravya* (mass or matter) and in this aspect it is eternal and indestructible.[3]

Helārāja, in explaining the view of Patañjali as expressed in the *Vākyapadīya*, says that since matter is the common element in all individual material objects it is difficult to define its nature except by the indefinite designations of 'this' or 'that'.[4] In another place in the *Vākyapadīya*, *dravya* is described as the unspeakable entity.[5] The appearance or manifestation of qualities is said to be due to the existence of differences in the constitution of that essence of things by virtue of which we call them matter. In another place it is said in the second *adhyāya* of the *Mahābhāṣya* of Patañjali that which is the principal agent which renders the accomplishment of action or motion possible is *dravya.* Helārāja explains it by saying that matter (*dravya*) possesses the energy or power (*śakti*) which renders actions possible.

The relation of matter and energy is one of great importance and we shall touch this point a little later. The followers of the Vaiśeṣika school of thought describe it as the entity in which all effects, actions and qualities inhere. It is regarded as a centre of passivity or non-opposition to the sequences of cause and effect, or, in other words, the *dravya* is regarded as that which stands as the basis of all cause and effect. It is eternal and indestructible. Śrīdhara, in his *Nyāyakandalī*, describes matter as possessing not only motion but inertia in motion (*vega*) which he regards as a specific quality different or distinct from motion. Raghunātha Śiromaṇi, in his *Padārtha-tattva-nirūpaṇa*, describes matter as that which is the permanent and undissociable seat of vibration.

In the above views of matter, which are more or less similar, atoms are regarded as the smallest particles that possess the necessary characteristics of matter—be it mass, persistence amidst change, adhesiveness, cause and effect of all changes, intertia or vibration.

The Buddhists proceeded on quite another line in their conception of matter. They conceived that corresponding to each variety or diversity of sensation, there was a real which affected us. These reals did not consist in any compounded form so as to form one connected whole, but they proved their existence by their diversity of effects as manifested in the diversity of sensations. We are ourselves aware only of a number of sensation-points and apart from these sensation-points or effect-producing reals, there is no proof that there exist many wholes or objects such as untrained common sense leads us to suppose. It is these sensation-points, mass-points or real-points, that owing to their multitudinous effects produce in us the impression of continuous mass or whole. The sensation of mass-points as continuous whole is due to their occupation of space; but there is no proof that mass as a whole is continuous. The notion of grossness or continuity as a whole is more or less a psychological error due to the simultaneous presentation in sensation of many discrete mass-points. These mass-points have, of course, different characteristic powers in accordance with which they can differently affect the different senses.

Vasubandhu, a great Buddhist thinker, holds in his *Abhi-*

dharmakośa Śāstra that each unit of the real represents a unit possessing the potential capacity of affecting our four senses as colour, smell, taste and touch and *paramāṇu* (atom) is the smallest particle of *rūpa*. It cannot be pierced through or picked up or thrown away. It cannot be placed anywhere or trampled or seized or attracted. It is neither long nor short, nor square, nor round, neither curved nor straight, neither high nor low. It is indivisible, unanalysable, invisible, inaudible, unlastable and intangible. By itself a *paramāṇu* (atom) is imperceptible. It becomes perceptible only when it combines with other *paramāṇus*. The perceptible atomic unit is not a *paramāṇu* but an *aṇu*, which is a combination of seven *paramāṇus* in a group in which there is one at the centre and four on four sides, one above and one below. The size of an atom is said to be $\frac{1}{1977326743}$ of a finger joint (or roughly a little less than an inch). The component of all things are directly these *paramāṇus* and not other wholes made out of them. Though the characteristics of all atoms are the same, yet some have certain of these characteristics as a potential energy and others as actual (kinetic). Accordingly, although all material things have the quality of the four elements, it happens that certain elements in one case display active energy while the others possess but a potential energy which does not act. The different characteristics which lie in the potential form may be actualised under suitable collocations.[6]

The Sāṅkhya theory which we shall discuss in some detail in the second part holds matter as being the combination of super-subtle mass-units and energy-units.[7] These combinations of mass-units and the energy-units are so collocated by their natural tendency into five kinds of infra-atomic potentials that there again by further fresh accretion of mass, develop themselves into five kinds of gross matter. The mass-units and the energy units are inseparable from one another and all varieties in matter are due to the unequal aggregation of mass and energy. What we call qualities or properties of matter are not different from the matter to which we think them attached, but are identical with them. Thus all mass-units are also conceived as tending to indicate heaviness (*guru*) or weight.

The Jains in discussing the nature of matter and their properties hold that from some point of view matter alone may be regarded as real, whereas the properties or qualities may be regarded as different manifestations of matter itself. Besides, from another point of view qualities alone may be regarded as existing. According to the latter point of view, it may be urged that all that affect us are but the phenomena of qualities. Where is the thing which may be said to exist beyond these phenomena of actions and qualities? Some new qualities come in, some remain permanent and some pass away, but not so the things themselves. A thing is never found either as permanent, produced or perishing, for it is a mere fiction, a mere airy nothing. We have never found a thing as producing a quality though the conglomerations of qualities are often illusorily supposed as things. Whatever we experience are but qualities. According to the former point of view, things alone, such as gold, silver, etc. exist, the qualities have no existence apart from them. It is the things that remain permanent and suffer changes of qualities, yet remaining permanent in themselves. The qualities cannot be regarded as having any independent existence apart from the things to which they are supposed to belong. It is only by illusory linguistic usage that we say that the things are said to possess qualities; in reality, however, these have the same identical existence as the things themselves.[8] According to the Jains, it is impossible to assert the reality of either matter or qualities to the exclusion of the other. From some point of view matter exists and from other points of view the qualities also exist; it is not also possible to reduce them to some higher category of reality which alone could be said to be real. Matter (*pudgala*) exists both in the atomic state as well as in compound forms (*skandha*) where two or more atoms combine together in groups. But contrary to the general Hindu conception of four kinds of elements, the Jains speak of each atom as possessing all the four characteristics of touch, taste, colour and smell. There is no classification of atoms as those that primarily give us touch (the wind atom), those that give us touch and colour (the light or heat atom), those that give us touch, colour and taste (the water atom), those that give us touch, colour, taste and smell (the earth atom); but each of the atoms is regarded as having all these four characteristics. As regards the diversity of taste, colour, smell and touch it is held that an atom possesses only one kind of taste, colour, smell, and two kinds of touch which are not mutually contradictory. Thus though an atom could have only one kind of taste, colour, smell (bad or good), one kind of colour (or one of the five primary colours, viz. black, blue, yellow, red and white),[9] one kind of taste out of the five kinds of primary taste (viz. bitter, pungent, astringent, sour and sweet) and two kinds of non-contradictory touch (e.g. oiliness and hot, oiliness and cold, rough and hot, rough and cold). The four elements—earth, water, fire and wind—are but the four kinds of bodies of souls in the lowest stage of development and they are formed by the combination of atoms of *pudgala*. These atoms are regarded as the ultimate causes and considered apart from the changes of qualities that their combinations are continually undergoing they may be considered as eternal in themselves.

The Nyāya-Vaiśeṣika also believes in the atoms, but in their theory the atoms of four classes such as air, light, water and earth are characterised respectively by touch, touch-and-colour, taste-colour-and-touch, colour-taste-touch-and-smell. Though in their atomic forms they do not show any of these qualities, these are manifested only when they combine together in molecular forms called the *trasareṇus*. It is indeed needless to mention that wind, light, water and earth do not mean in any of the Indian system the ordinary wind, light, etc. But these, according to them, stand as the principles which can affect the senses of touch, sight, taste and smell. These atoms of the Vaiśeṣikas had all-rounded forms without any specific manifest qualities, though even in the atoms of the same class it was held that there were specific differences by which any one of them could be recognised as different from the other by Yogins or men with superhuman powers of perception. The Jains dispensed with the classification of atoms into four classes and regarded that all atoms possessed the characteristics of touch, taste, smell, etc., but with them also these qualities could not be manifested in the atomic stages; the atoms also combined together in groups in different spatial orders and thereby manifested different kinds of touch, taste, light, heat and smell. There was no other separate whole apart from the groupings of these atoms as the basis of different kinds of touch, taste, etc. in diverse spatial orders.[10] The same atoms which by their conglomeration manifest a definite kind of colour may manifest quite any kind of taste, touch, smell and form. The forms of these molecular combinations may be straight, triangular, cubical, spherical and ellipsoidal.[11] These combinations may again be either dense or thin. Besides, these combinations may be such that the atoms display a monovalent or a divalent tendency. Thus we may have one combination with one atom in the middle and four others on four sides or by placing four atoms on each of the four sides. A combination having any of the five geometrical forms mentioned above may manifest any kind of colour, taste, etc. by reason of their varying degrees of density, or thinness or movement and divalent tendencies. About the condition under which the atoms may combine, it is said that combinations only take place between oily and rough atoms. But if the oiliness or roughness in the case of any atom is at a very low state or if they are of equal intensity in each of the combining atoms, no combination takes place. An oily atom is combined with another atom having double its oiliness; so also in the case of rough atoms; but a rough atom may be combined with another atom having oiliness of the same degree of intensity.[12]

Quite distinct from these atomic theories of the Nyāya-Vaiśeṣika, Sāṅkhya-Yoga, the Jains and the Buddhists is another theory of matter which was probably as old as any of these, but which began to be revived with some emphasis from the 9th century downwards and which received a clear utterance about the 12th century A.D. from the great Vaiṣṇava follower of Rāmānuja, namely, Veṅkaṭanātha Deśika.

Veṅkaṭa held that there was one primal matter undifferentiated in itself and partless. This is sometimes called *māya* since it could produce a diversified creation, sometimes called *prakṛti* (matter) for the evolutes that it can produce. It has been designated as partless in the sense that it is not made up of small parts such as the atoms or the like, but it may still be conceived that it undergoes some kind of changes in some portion of it and other kinds of changes at other portions of it and can differentiate itself by its inherent energy by the will of God, into diverse space, time and object relations. The theory that these are atoms which by their combination make up all things is untenable for there is no evidence that there are such partless indivisible atoms, possessed of no manifest qualities as the Vaiśeṣika supposes. Small particles or atoms may be admitted to exist only so far as they may be actually experienced, as in the dust particles floating in the air as reflected in the sun's rays coming through a chink or as may be inferred by smell which indicates that there must be small invisible particles floating in the air which contribute to the smell. But apart from these, there is no proof of the existence of such atoms as the Vaiśeṣika admits. The argument that divisibility of matter must have an ultimate limit does not prove the existence of atoms beyond the ken of experience, for we may take those small particles which may be experienced as our ultimate limit of divisibility. If divisibility would be allowed to extend *ad infinitum*, then it has to be supposed that since a mustard seed and a mountain are both liable to infinite division, the difference of size between them too would vanish from our consideration, for both of them are composed of an infinite number of atoms and no one can conceive of a difference between the one infinite and the other.[13] Moreover, the objections that have always been made against the atomic theory that if the atoms have parts they must be further divisible and if they have no parts they cannot come in contact with one another have great force in rejecting this doctrine of the Vaiśeṣikas. If after the Buddhist fashion a regular compounding of the atoms is not admitted still then the Buddhist theory of admitting the conglomeration or rather filing up of the atoms (*puñja*) would also require that the atoms must be occupying some space and this would naturally presuppose that the atoms have some dimension and hence parts. So it is better to admit that there was originally an undifferentiated, unmanifested, subtle mass which was variously called *avyakta*, *akṣara*, or *tamas*. In this original matter there arose undulatious or transformations in a series of stages as indicated by the Sāṅkhya which led to the production of all gross things, their combinations and compounds. The *tanmātras* (what the Sāṅkhya calls infra-atomic potentials) represent the stage of *prakṛti* just before it curdles into the state of the gross matter. *Ākāśa*, according to Veṅkaṭa, is a substance which is the seat of some kinds of sounds and gives room for all motion. Light is regarded as that kind of substance which is partless, having velocity and energy; and it manifests itself in association with lamps, the sun, etc. In accordance with the source from which it springs forth, it can serve different functions such as that of drying, increasing, cooking by chemical heat (*pāka*) and illuminating. Velocity is inseparably connected with it and this produces constant changes in its state. A ray of light is said to remain contracted or expanded according as it is obstructed or unobstructed. The light-substance performs various functions of drying, expanding, heating (in the sense of producing chemical changes) *according as the sources from which it is derived* varies.[14] This difference in the constitution of the light-heat substance as performing different functions is often referred to in some detail by the Nyāya school of thought, which also apparently prefers to think of light-substance as corpuscles emitted from a flaming source. Thus Govardhana in speaking of the change of colour, taste, smell and touch in objects by *pāka* says that *pāka* means the combination of different kinds of heat: there is one class of light-substance which generates different kinds of colour, there is another class which generates taste, another class which generates smell and another class which generates touch. Thus according to the diversity of effects different kinds of *pāka* (heat) are to be inferred. Some mangoes, e.g. put under a pile of grass change their green colour into yellow, but not so their sour taste which remains just as before. There are other mangoes which in spite of their green colour change their sour taste into sweet. Therefore, the heat that generates colour is different from that which generates taste. So that which generates smell is also thought as different. Even when the colour and taste remain the same, the old smell is often found destroyed by a new class of heat and a new kind of good smell is generated. So by heat hard touch of things is often destroyed kinds of *pāka* (heat) for generating different kinds of colour, taste, etc. So it is that the earth atoms, though of the same kind, are often found as appearing in different forms by the influence of *pāka*. Thus when the grass eaten by cows are broken up into atoms and a special type of heat changes its old taste, colour, touch and smell into such forms as these that belong to milk, and this special type of heat is such that exists in milk and conditions all its characteristic colour, taste, etc. These atoms form into dyad molecules (*dvyaṇukas*) and these again into *tryaṇukas*. The same of kind of process is repeated at the time of the transformation of milk into curd or from curd into butter.[15] This theory that there were different classes of heat-light rays to affect different kinds of change of characteristics of taste, colour, etc. is probably an original contribution of Govardhana himself, who seems to have lived not earlier than the sixteenth century. None of the earlier authorities such as Praśastapāda, Śrīharṣa, Śaṅkaramiśra, Jayanta, Vācaspati, etc. mention it. The only fact that they mention is that heat disintegrates the molecular structure of things into atoms and generates new characteristics in them and further helps them to combine together to form new molecules and their gross combination, on account of which the things so formed possess the changed qualities which were brought in the combining atoms by heat. The Nyāya does not believe in the disintegration of things into atoms by heat, but holds that the rays penetrate into the substances through their poral interstices and produce the change. The Nyāya and Vedānta also speak of the light rays as giving the power of penetrating through glass and water and also of penetrating through an impervious vessel and of heating things placed upon it.[16] It is also found in the *Vārttika* that ray of light could be reflected back from the surface of a mirror and thus could generate an image which was regarded as unreal by the Vedāntists like Apyayadīkṣita in his *Siddhāntaleśa*. This image could be seen in the prolongation of the direction in which the reflected ray reached the eye.[17] The ray is sometimes spoken of as taking a bent course too as we find hinted as in Uddyotakara's *Vārttika* and *Siddhāntaleśa*.[18] But these references are only occasional remarks made in connection with the visibility of objects in spite of the obstruction by transparent objects and not due to any regular investigation into reflection or refraction as treated in the modern text-books of physics. Their scientific value cannot therefore be considered to be of great importance. I only refer to these in order to come at a right conception about the Nyāya notion of light. It appears that light was conceived sometimes as the visible ray of light, sometimes as that which was visible as well as tangible in giving the sensation of heat, sometimes as being neither tangible nor visible. Thus the *tejas* or the light-heat substance was regarded as existing in four different forms.[19] *Tejas* substance is said to be existing ultimately as atoms or corpuscles; they all possess both heat and white colour, but the heat and colour may exist either in potential unmanifest forms (*anudbhūta*)[20] or in actual and manifest forms (*udbhūta*). Nyāya-Vaiśeṣika believed that the *tejas* existed stored up in the world etc. on account of which all *pāka* changes (chemical changes by heat in the organic nature) take place.

Veṅkaṭa believed that heat existed in a potential form in world etc., on account of which they could burn.[21] *Tejas* is said to exist in four sources in the Nyāya-Vaiśeṣika: (*i*) in the sun, meteors, electricity of the clouds, etc., (*ii*), as present in all earthly things such as wood, etc., (*iii*) as body heat producing all metabolic changes in the body, beginning with the digestive process and (*iv*) as heat underneath the surface of the earth in the mines transforming the earth atoms into the metals such as gold, etc.[22] The intense velocity of *tejas* is also noticed by Vācaspati, who describes it in the following words: on account of extreme lightness the velocity of *tejas* is simply unthinkable; as soon as the sun rises on the peak of the eastern hill immediately light enters into the houses.[23]

From the above considerations we see that light and heat were considered to be the same entity, though sometimes they could have an unmanifested form as well. This light-heat substance was considered by Nyāya-Vaiśeṣika as corpuscles which were emitted from their source of conglomeration whereas the Vaiṣṇava school, who did not accept the atomic theory, regarded it as a subtle thing by itself, which, by its different kinds of modification, manifested different kinds of heat and light.

We have indeed strayed far away from our consideration of the conception of matter. We have seen that Patañjali who represents the grammar school of thought had a fairly developed conception of mass though he did not at the same time deny the existence of individual material objects as such. One of the definitions of mass given by him was that it was that on account of which the things showed their tendency towards heaviness. In the atomic doctrines of Nyāya-Vaiśeṣika, heaviness and lightness are regarded as separate qualities on account of the possession of which things fall down or rise up. But Veṅkaṭa differed from the Nyāya-Vaiśeṣika view and held that *gurutva* or heaviness was nothing but the tendency of things (*svabhāva*) to fall. But this heaviness is not a separate quality of things but was identical with their nature. This tendency is inherent in the nature of things and represents but their very nature and is not therefore to be regarded as a separate quality. Things must fall if they are not in any way obstructed in realising this tendency. That some things fall with greater or lesser vehemence was due to their greater or lesser relative density or accumulation of mass. If heaviness (*gurutva*) is to be regarded as a separate quality of things owing to the possession of which things fell down then the curvilinear motion of air and the upward rise of burning flames have to be regarded also as separate virtues. Veṅkaṭa in corroboration of his views refers to *Nyāyatattva* in which it is said that heaviness is of three kinds, existing in water, fire and air, making them fall downwards, rise upwards or float in a parallel plane respectively. But then the question comes that if heaviness as a tendency to fall downwards belongs to the very constitution of matter itself why then should it be a characteristic of only the two elements, earth and water? The Nyāya-Vaiśeṣika thinks that heaviness is a quality which belongs to earth and water atoms. But Veṅkaṭa says that the Vaiṣṇavas may as well give the same kind of answer that it is only natural that the constitution of water and earth should be such that this would tend to fall downwards; this is all the more reasonable since, according to the Vaiṣṇava view, earth is but a transformed stage of the watery state; so if heaviness is defined as a tendency inherent in the constitution of matter, it is but natural to expect that though belonging to water it was transferred to earth when the former was transformed into the latter. If heaviness is not viewed as a potential power we may consider it as being identical with the thing itself looked at from a special point of view; if it is regarded as a special kind of power then one may regard it as a special manifestation of it determining all the phenomena of gravitation and as inhering in matter. Anyhow it is quite unreasonable to think of heaviness as an independent quality different from matter but inhering in it and causing it to fall as lightness existing in things as its other counterpart is regarded as causing things to rise up. Heaviness or lightness is not a separate and independent quality but is rather the mass of the thing or its special kind of constitution. Differences of heaviness were due to the relative density or conglomeration of mass.[24] It is indeed interesting to notice in the *Mahābhāṣya* of Patañjali, the grammarian who seeks to give a reason as to why through heaviness things tend to fall on the ground, which bears some similarity to Aristotle's doctrine of 'natural places' of things. Thus Patañjali says that a stone thrown upwards goes on with great velocity for a while, after which it does neither move parallel to the ground nor goes up, but being an earthy product comes to the earth, for it is with earth that it has got the greatest affinity.[25]

Apart from the above considerations regarding the substance of matter, there is another view of matter the seeds of which are found elaborated by Bhartṛhari in his *Vākyapadīya* and Helārāja in his commentary on it. It is said there that all things are but the conglomerations or collections of power or energy (*śakti*). These energies are of various kinds, some are natural but can be obstructed by human efforts, some exist only in a potential state and are only manifested in proper time. Things or objects are but conglomerations of such diverse kinds of energy or power and it is in accordance with the manifestation of any kind of such powers that a thing is said to be an agent as conducing to the accomplishment of any kind of action. If a thing could be spoken of as the agent of any action then the thing being the same there could only be but one kind of action. Therefore it has to be admitted that a thing is but the conglomeration of diverse kinds of powers or energies and in accordance with the setting free of some kind of power or energy the thing can behave differently as different agents. To speak of things and their energies is but a confusion of language for these are really the conglomerations of energies that being hypostatised behave as things.[26] In another chapter of the *Vākyapadīya* it is held that all these forces conglomerating as the objects of the world are but manifestations or modifications of one supreme force which is at once the ultimate principle of mind and matter of the universe.[27] The same idea occurs in a slightly modified form in *Spandapradīpikā*,[28] a treatise on Śaiva philosophy. Thus Utpala quoting from *Rahasya-Śāstra* says that there are two ultimate things in the world and the controller of them is the great God.

We have now considered some of the typical theories of matter as conceived by some of the leading schools of Indian thought. These were not mere passing conjectures, which had only an interest of the moment but these were necessary deductions from the fundamental principles of metaphysics and particular ways of looking at the problems of the world. The object of grammar is to explain our commonsense notions of things as they are expressed in language. Philosophy of grammar should therefore attempt to analyse the commonplace concepts of things until it could find some solid basis behind the shifting and often apparently conflicting modes of expression of the human mind as manifested in language presupposes an unconscious or semiconscious opinion about the true nature of the realities around us and their mutual relations. A philosophy of grammar should try to discover these by criticism. The results that it achieves is not generally a complete and systematic construction of our experience giving a consistent solution of all interrelated problems for in using language we do not try to construct a consistent whole of all the different parts of our experience; we simply take a fact of experience, look at it from a certain point of view and try to give expression to it. Philosophy of grammar may classify these points of view, which may or may not be related to one another and ascertain the philosophical basis presupposed in our commonsense expressions. In our ordinary ways of thinking we do not try to construct a system consistent in all its aspects. Thus we see that Patañjali, the great commentator of Pāṇini, gave at one time a notion of mass as the inherent essence of matter or the abiding principle which is the cause of the phenomenon of gravity; at another time when looking at things as agents in relation to action he conceived all objects as but conglomerations of powers or energies; at other times when he looked at things from the point of view of universals, genuses or types of things, he conceived matter as one unchangeable substratum. These points of view are not indeed reconciled by him but he shows us that when we look at things from different points of view in the course of estimate of things in connection with our linguistic expressions we may form different conceptions of matter.

Again the Nyāya-Vaiśeṣika conceived of the structure of things as being composed of atoms and regarded qualities, actions, etc. as having independent existence just as we often suppose them in our ordinary uncritical dualistic modes of experience. Following their general principle of metaphysics, the Nyāya-Vaiśeṣika has to define matter as that which is the seat of all qualities, movements and relations. There are different kinds of matter-atoms according to Nyāya-Vaiśeṣika and these are the seats of certain definite qualities; when these atoms combine the substance formed is regarded as undefinable and characterless for the first moment at which it is produced; thus the essential characteristic of matter, though undefinable, is such that it has the capacity or fitness to be the seat of diverse characteristic movements etc. The mathematicians who also took a commonsense view of things advocated this view. Thus Bhāskara says that though matter did not always contain qualities, and though capacity of possessing the qualities does not constitute the essence of matter and though therefore it is hard to characterise matter, yet the association of qualities is a condition of matter only in the sense that if qualities are to inhere in anything they must do so in matter. The Jaina philosophy was opposed to admitting the finality of any estimate of things. Sāṅkhya did not distinguish between substantive entities or matter and the qualities; it therefore regarded matter as super-infra-atomic substances, the mode of the manifestations of which appear as qualities. These super-infra-atomic substances which form the composition of matter have for their main constituents mass-units and energy-units by a mutual combination of which all material objects come into being. All manifest qualities and motions existed in these substantive entities in a latent form in such a manner that it was not possible to have a separate notion of qualities, etc. apart from these entities. Energy-units were separate from mass-units but they were so inseparably related together that none of them could exist independently of the other. Gravity was a direct product of the energy units. But by their joint product and varied collocations, combinations and recombinations, forces were let loose which manifested and actualised many qualities and characteristics of things which had remained hidden in a potential form. The process of evolution as conceived by this school of thought will be dealt with in some detail in the next part. The Vaiṣṇavas followed an old religious tradition that out of God, the principle of matter, called variously *prakṛti* or *māyā*, came forth and that it was upheld and maintained also by Him. All matter with them is thus one subtle principle which by diverse local congealings, undulations or modifications, resolved itself into diverse kinds of matter and their combinations, the material objects. As an example of how different kinds of material phenomena were accounted for according to these two different views of matter, the Nyāya-Vaiśeṣika and the Vedānta introduced the problem of the phenomenon of light and referred to the manner in which it was explained by them. Roughly speaking, we thus find that there was an atomic (Nyāya-Vaiśeṣika, Jaina, and Buddhist) and also, a super-infra-atomic theory of matter (Śāṅkhya-Yoga). There was the further theory that matter was a super-subtle indivisible essence much more subtler than other but in some sense comparable to it. Further, there was also the theory that matter was nothing but energy hypostatised as the individual objects, which only represented the collocative centres of different kinds of stress and strain of this matter and their individual actions meant only the letting loose in kinetic forms of some of the potential energies. Original matter may, from this point of view, be regarded as one ultimate substance or fund of energy. Matter was regarded as the background or substratum of all characteristics and qualities, etc. The Nyāya-Vaiśeṣika regarded the characteristics to be essentially different from matter and only attached to matter-combinations by an inseparable relation of inherence; the Sāṅkhya-Yoga regarded the characteristics to be but mere actualisations of potentials inherent in the super-infra-atomic groups of the *guṇas*; the Jaina did not regard qualities to be different from matter but conceived the latter to be eternally possessed of the qualities; the Tāntrikas, Śaivas and an alternative phase of thought in the Grammar School regarded matter as hypostatised energy and its qualities or characteristics as but its actual kinetic manifestations; the Vaiṣṇava view as represented by Veṅkaṭa showed that the characteristics were but the results of later developments through the congealing of the one essential subtle substance.

Turning now to the concept of motion we may begin with the curious nihilistic dialectic of the Buddhist Nāgārjuna (second century A.D.) who sought to prove that motion was an inconceivable, undeterminable, inexplicable *Nothing*, which produced only a so-called illusion of motion. Motion, he argued, cannot be anywhere, for motion can only be conceived as the tranversing of number of successive space-points, one after the other, as motion in space; but we see that motion can neither remain at the point which is just passed nor at the point which will be passed at a future succeeding moment. For the point which is traversed and passed no longer possesses any motion and the point which still remains to be passed has not been as yet associated with motion at all. Motion cannot also be in the thing which moves for it is only a collocation of atoms. The motion of a thing only involves the leaving off of a point and the taking of another. But as motion cannot belong to any point which has been passed or to the point which has to be passed at future moment, so also the space over which the motion takes place cannot be regarded as associated with motion, for the space which is associated with motion would require two motions, one associated with the space and the other involved in it of some other mover and this is impossible since there is only one mover. If the space is not associated with movement and is still called 'moving' or 'movable' then it becomes self-contradictory. If the movement is in the motion only then also the space unconnected with motion cannot have any association with motion. The one agent cannot be making the space moving as well as moving himself.

It cannot also be argued that motion rests on the mover, for if there is no motion then there is no mover and there are no two such motions so that one of which might inhere in the mover and the other exist as the motion. If it is held that it is on account of the association of movement that a mover is so called then even when a man thinks of moving without actually stirring his limbs, he may still be called a mover. Truly speaking, however, when we say that a mover moves we expect two movements, one in the mover and other in the movement, for the motion that makes a mover a mover cannot be the same as the motion that is accomplished by him in space. Again, if a motion is at all to begin, it must do so somewhere, but the point or points of space in association with which motion is conceived are either unmoved or but only moved and passed, and it is evident that in none of these do we find the motion beginning to set up itself, for the beginning of the motion must be a thing of the present but the points noticed in connection with motion are only the past and the future points. And since the motion is not found as beginning anywhere it is useless to speak of points which are passed or which remain to be passed. Again it is difficult to understand the relation between the mover and the movement; if the mover and the movement are one and the same then there would be no distinction of the agent and the action; if they are different then we should expect to have motion without the mover. Again that motion by virtue of which a mover is so called is not the same movement which the mover is said to undertake and accomplish. A mover is said to exist even before his movement actually begins; he is thus evidently not a mover by actually undertaking the motion. As has already been noticed the motion involved in the motion of a mover is not the same as the mover is associated with at the time of actually performing the motion; the two motions can hardly be formed by one agent. There is thus neither the motion nor the mover nor the moved. In the *Māhābhāṣya*, Patañjali (150 B.C.) anticipated these nihilistic objections discussed the notion of motion as follows: 'What is action? Attempt. What is an attempt? An effort. What is an effort? A movement. This is merely a series of synonyms, you cannot give a definite notion or picture as to what action is. Action is absolutely invisible, it is not a mass of matter that it can be shown to anybody. It can only be known by inference. What is the nature of such an inference? Here even, when all the accessories are present, sometimes the cooking takes place whereas at other times it does not take place. That by which Devadatta being here can also be at Pāṭaliputra is called an action.' In another place an action is said to be of six kinds: being produced, existing, changing, growing, decaying and being destroyed; these are all actions, only their modes are different. Action involved in being has one mode and that in dying has another. Again in connection with the possibility of a present movement he says that action alone can limit action, and 'present' only means the want of discontinuity of an action or an action which is one begun but not stopped. In fact, action is always going; it only so happens that some form of it is obstructed, hidden or veiled by other forms in consequence of which we speak of things as having passed away, or as remaining yet to come. Patañjali quotes the views of some who hold that there is no present movement, nothing falls, the rivers do not flow into the ocean, but apart from all relation to time all things are existing, unchangeable in themselves and there is no change or motion and he who even perceives this truth is really enlightened, not to speak of him who has thoroughly realised it in life. A young philosopher who considers himself wise asks a crow to define its flying; it cannot have flying defined as an action of a future moment; it cannot have it defined as a thing of the past, for when the action is past and gone the crow is but one with itself and there is no action on its part. If flying is an event of the present moment then all the world might as well be thought of as flying for there cannot be any movement limited to the point of a moment in the present. The future, past and present motion cannot exist in any of these, and therefore it is meaningless to speak of motion. The effort for the thing for which an action begins is only roughly spoken of as motion. The answer to this is that motion exists at the present moment though it cannot be perceived. The sun moves always but yet its motion cannot be perceived, so fine and subtle it is. So it is in the case of all motion. The fact that an action may be accomplished by the assemblage of accessories leads us to infer that the action which is accomplished in the course of some time must be continuing even at the present moment; so action in the present moment, though unperceived, may be inferred. Coming to the question of force and its distribution it is held by the *Mahābhāṣya* (as represented by Bhartṛhari and Helārāja) that things can generate action or motion not by themselves but by virtue of the energy or power (*śakti*) which inheres in them and not by themselves only, for things are inert in themselves and are unable to produce actions. Things as apart from the energies that inhere in them are incapable of any increase or decrease, or any variation which can be effectual at one time and ceases to be so at another. Thus looked at things appear as but conglomerations of energy (*śakti-samāhāra-mātraṃ ghaṭādayaḥ*). These energies are of different kinds; some are such that they take place of themselves at times; some are such that they are only manifested in the capacity of oppositions to other powers; some are such that they are manifested only after a lapse of time. There being such differentiation in the mode of the operation of diverse energies, it is not difficult to understand why certain actions are limited to certain causes. These energies functioning themselves in diverse modes of operation are often looked upon as things taking part as agents in the performance of diverse actions. The manifestations of energies into the accomplishment of actions are always taking place and these are only imagined by us as forms of diverse relations—the subject, the object, the ablative, the dative, the locative or the like. In reality, however, in the forces themselves there are no such differentiations: the different kinds of energies are effectualising themselves into actions and are individually called but agents or accessories with reference to the main action in comparison to which they are but subsidiaries. The relations of the energies to the action are not spcificable for they in reality form but one whole. Our interpretation of them in diverse relations are but impositions of our own intellect and imagination. What is actually seen is falsely identified with what is imposed upon by the mind and this leads to the impression that action as happening outside is also limited in the manner in which the case relations are supposed to indicate. That an action sometimes appears as dependent on another or that it manifests itself in sequence or succession is but an imagination of our conceptual system of thought. In the action itself there are no such distinctions. This view, we see, holds that things themselves, which we remember, according to Patañjali, were but the mass, the background of all phenomena of gravity etc. held hidden within themselves different kinds of energy which under the influence of collocation of such other energies transformed itself into action. Everywhere there were but the various transformations of energy on the background of mass and the conception of sequence of action in successive moments, the agents of action, the objects and the like, are but merely imaginations of the mind imposed upon the entire order without critically examining how far this actually holds good there. Mass and energy are different yet in ordinary commonsense they are often loosely identified and this is responsible for the notions current amongst us that actions are generated by the mass or the thing.

In reality, however, the conception here expressed shows that mass or the thing is the inert, characterless something, whereas all characters and actions are due to the manifestations of diverse energies located in it. It is not possible to produce any change or transformation in the nature of the masses, the thing itself and the energies only lean upon the mass as a place of rest since they cannot remain without. When the accessories are there the things are moved and the energies are manifested.[29]

Another view is also mentioned in the *Vākyapadīya* in which it is said that the energy is flowing on like a stream and the mass conglomerations or rather individual energies of objects are like leaves and things floating on it. In reality, however, it is difficult to estimate the relation of mass and energy; but as the grammar school of thought is based upon commonsense conceptions as used in language it is to be held that they are different but related to each other. It may, however, be said that if the question is pressed towards the ultimate metaphysical borders, it will be seen that unity is not indeed different from diversity. It is the nature of Reality to express itself both as unity and diversity. That which is unquestionably diverse does not differ from unity and that which is unquestionably unity does not differ from diversity. Diversity and unity are but the modes in which the reality shows itself. It is therefore idle to try to come to a finality as to whether mass is the same as energy or different from it.

Kumārila, the great teacher of the Mīmāṃsā school of thought, regarded *śakti* (energy or power) as existing eternally; concussion, push, etc. only served to manifest it. The mass which is regarded as the place of support for the energy manifests it only when other suitable collocations or excitants take part. Manifestation of energy means relating the energy with the thing with which it is found associated. It is the nature of action that it is found to belong in that substance with which it comes in relation or in which it inheres; so manifestation of action means only relating it with a thing; that which is called an agent of action is only an agent which brings about the relation of the energy with the thing or retards and destroys it, but cannot destroy the action or the energy. In another place, Kumārila holds that in energy itself there is no difference but it is only inferred as being of different types or order according as the effect is found to be different. Difference in effect only leads us to infer different kinds of energies to explain the diversity and this gives rise to our conception of diverse kinds of energy. The differences in the production of the effect refer only to the differences in the way of relating the energy and do not presuppose an intrinsic difference in the nature of energy itself. For ordinary purposes however the energies may be conceived as different, each of which is specifically fit for producing a special kind of effect.

According to the Vaiśeṣika philosophy, *karma* or motion is

regarded as residing through a relation of inseparable inherence in the atoms. It is an ultimate concept in itself which is the cause of all contacts and disjunctions (*saṃyoga* and *vibhāga*). Each unit of motion is a momentary phenomenon involving the movement of an atom of its own unit of space, and thus causing conjunction or disjunction with other atoms. Motions classified according to different directions—such as upward, downward, contraction, expansion, rectilinear or curvilinear—are but all the same, viewed in relation to space. Motion is an ultimate and simple entity by itself; it is neither generated by any other simpler thing of its own class nor can it generate things in which it is found to inhere. The different kinds of upward or downward motion, or that of exit and entrance, are all due to its associations with other things which give us our notion of relative motion. The same motion which may appear to some as entrance, looking at it from a certain point of space, may appear to others, looking from other points of view, as exit. These relative motions are different from the five kinds of spatial motion such as upward, downward, etc. The relative motions are unreal, being only appearance, for at the same time there cannot be two different kinds of motion in a thing; the contradictory appearances of motion are therefore subjective appearances.

A unit of motion is as we have seen but that ultimate phenomenon which explains the displacement of an atom of its own unit of space. This unit of motion cannot generate further motion. But the continued pressure or impact (*abhighāta*) which generated the motion produce through it a *saṃskāra* or persistent tendency to motion (*vega*). It is this *vega* that is the cause of the motion of the thing in one definite direction (*niyata-dik-kriyā-prabandha-hetu*). A thing follows the same direction with reference to which the motion had generated the *vega*. This *vega* is destroyed by coming in contact with a dense thing which sometimes takes the motion itself. When the motion of the thing is very slow, the slightest obstruction to it by a thing is sufficient to arrest it. Thus when an arrow flies up to a great distance, its motion being very slow, is arrested by the obstruction of the motionless layer of the upper air. Motion thus generates one *vega* (impressed motion, momentum) which lasts till the cessation of motion. But the Nyāya supposes that there is a series of *saṃskāras* (momentum) each of which generates the one that succeeds it. The Vaiśeṣikas hold that the *vega*, once generated, goes on producing a series of motions for we must remember that one unit of motion is satisfied by causing the displacement of an atom of its own unit of space. It should be noted that *vega* is different from motion. *Vega* is a tendency, a quality of the thing which can generate motion and the motion again generates *vega*; thus *vega*, though it is but a tendency or quality of things, can yet generate motion. Quickness or slowness of motion is due to greater or lesser *vega*. The other view as taught in the Nyāya school holds that the first motion generated a motion and that another kind of *vega*, and that another *vega*, and so on. The Vaiśeṣika view holds, as we have already seen, that the *vega* once generated remains in greater or lesser proportion through the whole progress of the motion until the moved thing is arrested. The *vega* gradually exhausts itself while continuing to produce motion by overcoming opposition. When the power of the *vega* is reduced to a minimum, it cannot overcome even the opposition of still atmosphere; and this is what arrests the motion of an arrow after a long upward flight, when it falls back to the ground.

Gravity is the quality of things that brings them to the ground. Patañjali, the commentator of Pāṇini, regarded it as mere affinity of the earth to earthly things. Bhāskara regarded it as being due to the attraction of the earth on things. Things that fall from above to the earth begin their first unit of motion under the influence of gravity; the first moment of motion generates a *vega* and with this *vega* the force of gravity is added; this accelerates the motion. In the case of the upward flight of an arrow, it goes upwards only so long as its *vega* is sufficient to overcome the counteraction or opposition of gravity. Then the *vega* exhausts itself in its attempt to overcome the opposition or obstruction (*pratibandhakatā*) of gravity, then the object falls down to the ground.

If pressure or impact produces a motion in a direction opposite to that in which *vega* tends to produce the motion (as in the case of the rebounding of a club in thrashing corn) then as a result of the interaction of the two forces (viz. the *vega* and its opposition) the direction of the motion is changed. Some held that in such cases of rebounding the original *vega* was lost and a new upward motion was generated by the impact. Others held that the upward rebounding was the resultant of two opposing forces of the downward *vega* and the force of impact. The case of the rotatory motion has well been sketched from *Nyāyakandalī* by Dr. B.N. Seal. Each particle of the relating body, e.g. the potter's wheel has, at any given instant, a motion in a definite direction. The rotatory motion of the body results from the separate motions of the particles and their persistent tendencies, joined with the fact of the rigid conjunction of the particles. When the rod strikes one part of the wheel, the motion on the part struck is in the present instant produced by impact; while the other parts move through the transmission of force due to the rigid cohesion of parts. The subsequent motions in other parts are explained by their persistent tendencies and the transmission due to rigid cohesion. When the rod is disjoined from the wheel the rotatory motion continues, being due merely to the persistent tendencies in the constituent parts and the resultant persistent tendency in the whole.

Four classes of motion are described in the *Nyāyakandalī*: (*i*) Motion by *nodana* or continued pressure as in the case of the motion of an object pushed or pulled by the hand, of heavy stones sinking in the mud, of the arrow flung out of a bow-string, motion of volumes of clouds or sailing vessels. (*ii*) Motions produced by any sudden shock or impact (*abhighāta*) as in the case of a stone falling to the ground and breaking it and entering into the ground. (*iii*) Motion due to direct contact with an elastic body which exercises a moving force by means of elasticity in its tendency to return back to its original form as when a bent bow tries to retain its original straightness when it is relieved of its pressure. (*iv*) Where motion is conducted from one body possessing *vega* to another moving body by direct contact.[30]

It will be seen that the main difference between the Mīmāṃsā and the Nyāya view of motion consists in this that, according to the latter, motion is always some kind of *parispanda* or vibration causing the displacement of an atom of its own unit of space, whereas, according to the former, some non-sensuous *śakti* or energy or power is admitted. How originally motion is generated cannot be answered by Nyāya. According to Mīmāṃsā, however, *śakti* is the unknown cause of all motion or action.

According to Sāṅkhya, mass-reals and energy-reals are inseparably associated. In Nyāya-Vaiśeṣika, motion is an entity which inheres in the atoms. In Sāṅkhya, however, much beyond the atomic or even the infra-atomic stage the mass-units and the energy-units exist together in eternal association. These are indeed different from one another, but they always remain in association with one another. At the ultimate *prakṛti* stage, the mass-units and the energy-units so counterbalance one another that none of them can be manifested. This unmanifested unknown union of mass and energy holds within itself in potentiality all the later forms of development as matter or motion of diverse kinds. There is no actual *parispanda* at this stage for it is a state of perfect balance. It is indeed difficult to understand how mass can so oppose energy as to stop its manifesting powers. This mass however is beyond atoms or infra-atoms, beyond the powers of gravitation or anything else. It only stands for the Real which is acted upon by the energy Real. It is not one, but many; it therefore is conceived to be existing as infinitesimal Reals. These mass-reals and energy-reals are the causes of all world progress and change. A more elaborate examination of its doctrine of evolution will be described in the second part in connection with the theory of cosmic change.

Veṅkaṭa differs from Nyāya-Vaiśeṣika and Sāṅkhya in his conception of motion. He holds that motion or *karma* is that which produces the notion of movement. Veṅkaṭa does not also think, as Patañjali did, that motion is a thing which cannot be perceived, but can only be inferred.

It cannot be defined as that which causes displacement of anything generating corresponding conjunction and disjunction, but it is the one whole of movement producing a corresponding notion in us. It is perceived by us in the very moment of its existence. It has no other nature than that of a thing becoming dissociated from one place and associated with another. It is not momentary but a whole involving the spatial dissociation at one point and association at another. It is not an entity different from the thing but represents only a condition of it.[31]

Veṅkaṭa further does not agree with the Vaiśeṣika that there is a separate entity, *vega*, which is different from motion. Veṅkaṭa on the other hand holds that *vega* is only a mode of motion, such as 'It goes very quickly'. There is no other thing called *vega*.

That the difference of *vega* is due to the difference of motion is also admitted by the Vaiśeṣika. What is the use then of admitting *vega* as a separate tendency or entity? Its purpose may as well be served by admitting different kinds of motion. It is better to hold that the preceding action generates the later action and this process continues. This will dispense with the admission of any further extraneous *vega*. The generating of a succession of actions or motion may be held to be conditioned by the thing as much as one action. According to Veṅkaṭa, elasticity also is not regarded as a separate entity as is viewed by the Vaiśeṣika scholars. The phenomenon of elasticity is not different from the natural quality in things to remain in its own form or condition. Elasticity thus is not to be considered as a separate quality or entity but is the natural form of things, which when disturbed returns to itself.[32]

The Ionian philosophers of Greece had some conception of the indestructibility of matter and they sought to put forward the idea that all forms of matter could consist of one simple element such as air or fire, though without giving any definite reason. First to work out the doctrine of elements was Empedocles (c. 450 B.C.), who conceived the principles of the four elements: earth, water, air and fire. It was a hypothesis which served to interpret the phenomena of nature for many centuries till in modern days the growth of chemistry identified over seventy elements. But it seems that they too were searching for the proximate units of chemical action, though in their own way. In Greece the Eleatics denied all motion and change, declaring them to be illusions of the senses, while reason led us to perceive that alone which was unchangeable. Heraclitus found that this theory contradicted all experience and held that a continual change was taking place in the world. The Pythagoreans found this permanent element in number and entirely abandoned materialism. Leucippus and his disciple Democritus found the principle of matter in the atoms; these atoms were particles of matter so minute that they could not be further divided and were not perceptible to the senses; they were of varying sizes and form, but all consisting of the same substance or matter, which could not be more precisely defined. Particular things come into being when these atoms combine and disappear when they separate; but the atoms themselves are eternal and indestructible. The atoms are simple, impenetrable and indivisible; but these are not mathematical points or centres of force. Owing to the many different shapes of atoms—some having hooks, others eyes or grooves or humps or depressions—they interlace and combine together. These differences in the atoms that are responsible for the differences in bodies. They act on one another by direct contact only through pressure and impact and action at a distance is impossible. The atoms are in motion from the very beginning and this causes their union or separation. The atoms of Epicurus are indivisible not by nature but on account of their hardness.

The medieval philosophers no doubt thought of matter as composed of minute parts and they followed the ancient philosophers in regarding the parts as of four elements, fire, air, earth and water. Bacon held that the foure lements were made of *Hyle*, that each could be converted into the nature of another and everything into anything else (compare the Sāṅkhya doctrine of *sarvaṃ sarvātmakam*) everything is reducible to every other thing). The particles of Bacon however were not the atoms of Democritus, for he says in the *Novum Organum,* 'Not by this are we brought to the atom which presupposes vacuum and matter immutable (both of which are false) but true particles as they are found to be.' Bacon thought that between the particles there was an intangible weightless matter which he called 'Spirit'. It is important to note that Bacon was the first to regard heat as a mode of motion. Descartes discarded the indivisibility of atoms saying that however small we may imagine the parts we are always able in thought to divide any one of them into two or more smaller parts. He discarded vacuum as being repugnant to reasons and held all space to be filled up with matter. Sensible bodies are all composed of insensible particles of three elementary forms. The first element consists of very minute bits, of irregular shape and capable of very rapid motion; chips of the particles forming the second, the earth and the planets the third. The second and the third elements appear to have vortices of the first element round them and these vortices account for the forces which Descartes supposed to exist round the sun and planets to account for their orbital motion.

Robert Boyle (1627-1691) in his *Origin of Forms and Qualities* says that there are in the world great stores of particles of matter, each of which is too small to be sensible; and being entire or undivided, must needs have its determinate shape and be very solid. Though it be mentally or by divine omnipotence divisible yet by reason of its smallness and solidity, Nature never actually divides it; and these may in this sense be called *Minima* or *Prima Naturalis*. That there are also multitudes of corpuscles, which are made up of the coalition of the several of the former *Minima Naturalis* and whose bulk is so small and their adhesion so close and strict, that each of these little primitive concretions or clusters of articles is singly below the discernment of sense and though not absolutely indivisible by Nature into the *Prima Naturalis* that compose it, or perhaps into other little fragments yet, for the reasons freshly intimated, they very rarely happen to be actually dissolved or broken but remain entire in great variety of sensible bodies and under various forms or disguises. He discards the old elements air, earth and water, and says that these three are to be regarded as made up of mixed bodies which had been regarded as mixtures of air, earth and water and had so come to be called mixed bodies. He dwells on the idea that an enormous number of compounds may be made into various arrangements of corpuscles and that they differ from each other in nothing but the various textures resulting from the magnitude, shape, motion and arrangement of the small parts. Boyle thus agreed with Descartes in thinking of matter as one in kind, the differences being due solely to shape, size and motion of the parts. Newton was an experimental philosopher, who discovered laws by experiment and observation using mathematics to deduce consequences and comparing them with further experiment and observation thereby verifying or correcting the laws. He did not concern himself much with speculations about the ultimate structure of matter. But he was also a believer in the atomic theory and he says in his *Principia*, 'It seems probable to me that God in the beginning formed matter in solid, massy, hard, impenetrable, movable particles.' Bernouilli (1738) held that a gas consists of very minute corpuscles moving with great velocity in all directions and that the pressure of a gas against the walls of a containing vessel was due to the bombardment by these corpuscles. Boscovich in 1758 formulated his hypothesis that an atom is a central point to which mass or inertia is assigned; towards this mass-point force is acting so that another mass-point is urged towards it with an acceleration proportional to the mass of the first point and varying with the distance in such a way that at a great distance the attraction is inversely as the square of the distance. But when the distance becomes very small the force undergoes one or more alterations of repulsion and attraction, finally ending with a repulsion which is infinitely great when the two points are infinitely near each other. Two central mass-points can therefore never actually coincide. Boscovich's predecessors had like Newton imagined a hard nucleus round the centre of the atom; Boscovich showed that the nucleus was unnecessary. Its place was efficiently taken by the repulsive force rapidly increasing as the centre was approached. The nucleus had no part to play and might be discarded. Priestly (in his *Vision* 1772 and *Matter and Spirit* 1977) and Faraday adopted Boscovich's theory. Faraday laid stress on the uselessness of the little hard nucleus of finite size and urged that the powers of matter, the forces which it exerts, are all that we know about it. These powers or forces are the matter and where they extend the matter also extends. In recent years Lord Kelvin also took up the theory of Boscovich and sought to show how the grouping of Boscovichian atoms could account for crystaline arrangement and for phenomena of light. Poynting remarking on Boscovich's theory says that the theory of Boscovich though conceivable mathematically is rather difficult to be conceived physically. We think of force as effort symbolised by muscular effort. We must have a quality at least in thought. If we think of force we think also of that which the force moves or perhaps more fundamentally that which resists the force and we call this matter. If with Boscovich and Faraday we identify the moved with the mover and say that matter is but force, then we have a dual aspect of force. In one aspect it acts and in another it suffers action. Such a conception of the unity of matter and force and unity as force rather than as a matter, is a permanent contribution to philosophical ideas.

Side by side with the different speculations about the atoms, the theory of the four elements of the ancients was gradually being revived. About 1700 the phlogiston theory of Stahl was coming into fashion. This theory held that the metals contained a something called 'phlogiston' which they gave off on combining with air, that oxygen was air deprived of phlogiston, that nitrogen was air containing phlogiston itself. This theory was accepted by Black, Cavendish and Priestly. In 1789 William Higgins in his book *A Comparative View of the Phlogistic and Antiphlogistic Theories* held that water was composed of molecules formed by the union of a single ultimate particle of light inflammable air and that they are incapable of uniting to a third particle of either principle. Thus the four elements, fire, air, earth and water were gradually being destabilised from their supreme position. A number of gases was being discovered with definite properties and obviously not mere modifications of air. Air itself was found to consist almost entirely of two gases and so it ceased to be regarded as an element. Cavendish's discovery that water was a compound of Hydrogen and Oxygen removed it too from the list. Fire was however still regarded as a substance. Dalton published his *New System of Chemical Philosophy* in 1808 in which he expressed his views about the atomic theory. Dalton's contribution consists in the clearness of his conception of an element as consisting of particles all alike, and whether truly atomic or not, yet indivisible by ordinary chemical agency, and in his supposition that compounds consisted in general of small groups of these elementary particles or atoms. This gave an easily pictured hypothesis to account for the chemical fact, by this time established, that the elements combine in definite proportions, which are always integral multiples of the smallest proportions in which they enter into combinations. Soon after the publication of Dalton's theory Avogardro formulated the hypothesis that in gases at the same temperature and pressure equal volumes contain equal number of molecules.

A tendency was also growing that the atoms were really made of one kind of material. Thus Prout held that all the atomic weights were exact multiples of the atomic weight of hydrogen, a supposition which seems to imply that other elements were really but groups of hydrogen not to be divided by known agency. The kinetic theory first introduced in a rudimentary manner by Joule in 1848 (*Scientific Papers*, I. 290) was worked upon by Kronig, Claussius, Maxwell and Boltzmann. It supposes that a gas consists of an enormous number of molecules, all exactly alike in a given gas, but so small that their average distance apart is very great compared with the size of any one molecule. These molecules are flying about in all directions with very great velocities, continually colliding with each other and with the walls of any containing vessel. The greatest triumph of the kinetic theory consists in its determination of the size of the molecules and of the number in a given space. By the size of the molecules we are not to suppose some definite solid shape. We may imagine two molecules approaching so closely that they just begin to collide. Drawing equal spheres round each just touching the radius of either sphere is termed the radius of molecular action, and the sphere round each molecule is taken to be the size of the molecule even though the atomic centres may be far within the surface of the sphere. A relation can be found connecting the mean free path, the molecular size, and the number present in unit volume; and since the mean free path is known this gives a relation between size and number.

Since the kinetic theory of matter arose various speculations on the structure of atoms and molecules have been offered. Thus Rankine assumed that the atoms were little nuclei surrounded by atmospheres whirling round them in vortices—a revival of the Cartesian idea. Lord Kelvin following Helmholtz's investigations on fluid motion held that space is full of a frictionless incompressible fluid of uniform density throughout. An atom is a vortex ring in this fluid, a ring-shaped portion of the fluid distinguished from the rest solely by its peculiar whirling motion. We can make rings in real fluids, because they possess viscosity or friction. But in a frictionless fluid, the creation and equally the destruction of a ring would require forces to act which the fluid itself does not possess; so that a ring if in existence must have existed in all past time and will persist in all future time, the same portion of the fluid always existing in it. Here we have a suggestion of an indivisible or eternal atom. It also suggests the possibility that all energy is of one kind, energy of motion, either of the rings themselves or of the fluid outside the rings. Larmor (1897) supposes that space is filled with an elastic solid, or jelly, capable of vibrating and carrying waves. An atom is the centre of a strain or twist in the jelly. The strain is persistent; but it can move from point to point in the jelly using new parts as it travels along. It is the form of the strain which is the persistent atom.

The latest atomic hypothesis is one which assigns an electric current, a definite charge of electricity of each kind is required to disengage a definite amount of an element from a compound, and that, if we accept the atomic theory, the charge is proportional to the number of atoms disengaged. The hydrogen atom always requires the same charge. Other atoms require either the same charge as the hydrogen atom or twice the charge of a small multiple of it. It is therefore to be supposed that when we decompose a molecule, each constituent has a charge, one positive, the other negative, and we have to put in equal neutralising charges to render the products of decomposition neutral. This interpretation of Faraday's discovery may be regarded as the foundation of the theory of electrical atom. Crookes found out that in it in a space sufficiently rarefied discharge takes place between two metal plates, a steam of negatively electrified matter shoots straight out from the plate to which negative electricity is supplied. This stream of matter can be deflected by a magnet. Sir J.J. Thomson found that it can be deflected also by electric force. In a series of experiments on the deflections by known magnetic and electric forces he made the immensely important discoveries that the mass carrying a given charge is the same whatever the gas used, and that it is 1/1700 part of the mass of hydrogen which would carry the same charge. By further experiments he showed that each particle in the stream carried a charge equal to that of the hydrogen atom, so that the mass of each particle is 1/1700 part of the mass of the hydrogen atom. These minute carriers of negative electricity he termed 'corpuscles' which are more generally known as 'electron'. It has to be supposed that the electric forces during the discharge tear away the negatively electrified portions of the atoms at the negative plates, that these are all alike for all atoms, and that their mass is but 1/1700 part of the mass of the hydrogen atom. If the atom was neutral before the corpuscle was torn from it, an equal positive charge remains behind upon what is left. The electrical explanation of the atom consists of the supposition that an atom consists electrically of a charge of positive electricity and a greater or less number of electrons. There are reasons also for supposing that the number of electrons is proportional to the atomic weight. The oxygen atom possesses for instance 16 times as many electrons as the hydrogen atom. The positive charge is equal to the sum of all the negative charges on the electrons. This positive charge is supposed to be spherical and to be distributed uniformly within the sphere. The electrons are moving about inside the globe, and can move without resistance through the positive. It is possible that the mass of the electron is entirely due to its charge. Calculation shows that a massless sphere carrying a surface charge equal to that of the hydrogen atom, and about 10^{-13} cm in radius, would behave as if it had mass of the hydrogen atom. If we could suppose that the hydrogen atom contains 1700 electrons we could thus account for its whole mass. But it appears much more probable that atom contains but one or a few electrons, so that if we are still to give an electrical account of mass, we must break up the positive globe into very small spheres enormous in number, and each containing a very small charge, far smaller than that of the electron, these being scattered through the globe. All our measurements of energy involve the idea of mass, and it may perhaps be maintained that the magnetic energy in the space round the moving electron implies the existence of mass in that space to serve as a seat for the energy. If so the electric theory of mass only takes the mass from the inside of the moving sphere and spreads it through the outside space. Again we come to the Boscovich-Faraday conception that an atom is wherever its forces acts—not at the centre alone but spread through all space.[33]

If we compare the doctrines of the Greek atomists with those of the modern European scientists we see that the Greeks did not possess any of the detailed physical and chemical knowledge on which the present day atomic theory is based. The objects of Leucippus and Democritus were quite different from that of Dalton and Avogardro. To the latter the conception of atoms and molecules served as a means of explaining certain definite and detailed facts of chemical combination and gaseous volume in a more definite and exact way than any other hypothesis available at the time. To the Greek philosophers, the atomic theory was an attempt to make the universe intelligible. The atomic theory of the Greeks presents a consistent picture of nature within the limits of the knowledge of their day. It is easy to show where it fails in the light of the knowledge of phenomena we now possess, but the attempt to frame an intelligible picture was a great effort in advance, and a study of the flaws which we can now detect may serve to suggest the provisional nature of some of the theories by the aid of which knowledge is advancing so fast in our own day. But the great difference between the position of the Greeks and that of the modern time in regard to natural knowledge consists in the small number of phenomena known to them contrasted with the enormous wealth of accumulated observation which is available for us as the result of years of experiment with the aid of apparatus unknown to the ancients. When a new theory is put forward it is now almost always possible to test its concordance with facts by the use of material already accumulated or to suggest in the light of such material experiments which will serve to refute it or to lend it greater probability. To test a new theory in the ancient world other phenomena were rarely available than those which suggested it, or to explain which it was put forward. Thus thought was much more speculative and as is still the case with metaphysics, no general consensus of opinion was reached. Each philosopher had a system of his own in science, just as he still has in metaphysics.

The position of the speculations of the Indian sages on matter and motion is similar to that of Greece and unlike modern conditions in this that the facts on the observation of which their theories were based were incomparably smaller than what we observe in our days. In modern times, the facts of matter-relations that we observe from day to day are diverse and highly complicated; in order to generalise these facts, some theories have to be formed which can consistently explain them. These theories stand for a time and when any such fact is newly discovered as cannot be explained by them, they have to be revised, or forsaken. The theories formulated are based upon a very large number of facts and have as such a chance of stability. But the number of investigators employed in observing facts is numerous, the apparatus at their disposal are diverse as well as many, and as a result of that, there is every chance of new facts being discovered any moment which may throw overboard the most well-established theory that was current for a very large number of years. In former times, facts were observed by the naked eye without any apparatus and there was but little chance of the discovery of any such new facts which could upset a theory. The theories formulated in ancient times whether in India or in Greece had thus remained in force for a much longer time than the theories that are formulated in our own times. The method or manner in which Hindu theories of matter and motion formed was almost the same in which the scientific theories of modern times are formed. In Greece, there was only one type of atomic theory, viz. that formulated by Leucippus and conveyed to his disciple Democritus and later on adopted by Epicurus. This might as well be thought as the result of a happy guess inasmuch as Democritus employed his atomic theory not only in explaining the material world, but also in explaining psychology. But the Hindus had formulated diverse theories of matter and motion which, though crude in themselves for want of sufficient number of scientific facts, have their correlates or counterparts in a general way in the theories of modern science. There was thus different types of atomic theory, the energy theory of one subtle all-pervasive matter, by the undulations or congealings of which all other material objects were formed. As it appears, these theories were not mere lucky guesses. They were preceded by a careful analysis of our conception of matter in accordance with the ordinary facts of experience. In the hymns of *Ṛgveda* we first notice the beginnings of enquiry into the mystery of creation. It asks what was in the beginning, it doubts whether it was pure darkness or water that existed in the beginning; it suggests that it was probably a state which was so indeterminate that it might be called both existent and non-existent. In the Upaniṣads the doctrine of the five elements had become established and we find also that the subtler states of *tanmātra*, *mahat* and the primeval *prakṛti* are also referred to. The theory of the *guṇa*s of Sāṅkhya also seems to have been developing gradually in the Upaniṣads.[34] That ordinary material objects were the products of the transformation of some other finer states of existence and that the qualities of the material objects had developed by the combination of certain simple elements were already accepted as facts in many of the Upaniṣads. Thus in the *Chāndogya* we read that the great Being desired to become many and out of such a desire He created *tejas* (heat), the *tejas* desired to become many and created *ap* (water) and it is therefore that whenever anybody cries or sweats, water comes out on account of heat. *Ap* desired to become many and produced food, it is therefore that where there is rain there grows food; from water (*ap*) therefore grows the food. That Being (i.e. that which had produced fire, water, food [earth]) thought, let me now enter those three beings—fire, water, earth—with this living self (*jīvātman*) and let me then reveal names and forms. Then that Being having said 'let me make each of these three tripartite' (so that fire, water and earth should each have itself for its principal ingredient, besides an admixture of the other two) entered into these beings (*devatā*) with this living self only and revealed names and forms. He made each of these tripartite and said how these three beings become each of them tripartite. The red colour of burning fire is the colour of fire, the white colour of fire is the colour of water, the black colour of fire is the colour of earth. Thus vanishes what we call fire as a mere variety, being a name arising from speech. What is true are the three colours (or forms). The red colour of the sun is the colour of fire, the white of water and the black of earth. Thus vanishes what we call the sun, as a mere variety, being a name arising from speech. What is true are the three colours. The red colour of the moon is the colour of fire, the white of water and the black of earth. Thus vanishes what we call the moon as a mere variety, being a name arising from speech. What is true are the three colours. The red colour of the lightning is the colour of fire, the white of water, and the black of earth. Thus vanishes what we call lightning, as a mere variety, being a name arising from speech. What is true are the three colours. Great householders and great theologians of olden times who knew this have declared the same saying: 'No one can henceforth mention to us anything which we have not heard, perceived or known. Out of these (three colours or forms) they knew all, whatever they thought looked red, they knew was the colour of fire. Whatever they thought looked white, they knew was the colour of water. Whatever they thought looked black, they knew was the colour of earth. Whatever they thought was altogether unknown, they knew was some combination of those three beings (*devatā*). Now learn from me, my dear, how those three beings, when they reach man, become each of them tripartite. The earth (food) when eaten becomes threefold; its grossest portion becomes feces, its middle portion flesh, its subtlest portion mind. Water when drunk becomes threefold; its grossest portion becomes urine, its middle portion blood, its subtlest portion breath. Fire (i.e. oil, butter etc.) when eaten becomes threefold; its grossest portion becomes bone, its middle portion marrow, its subtlest portion speech. For truly my child mind comes of earth, breath of water and speech of fire.'

Later on Śvetaketu's father further advises Śvetaketu thus: 'Man (*puruṣa*), my son, consists of sixteen parts. Abstain from food for fifteen days but drink as much water as you like, for breath comes from water, and will not be cut off, if you drink water.' Śvetaketu abstained from food for fifteen days. Then he came to his father and said, 'What shall I say?' The father said: 'Repeat the Ṛk, Yajur and Sāma verses.' He replied: 'They do not occur to me, Sir.' The father said to him, 'As of a great lighted fire one coal only of the size of firefly may be left, which would not burn much more than this (i.e. very little), thus my dear son, one part only of the sixteen parts (of you) is left, and therefore with that one part you do not remember the Vedas. Go and eat. Thou wilt understand me.' Then Śvetaketu ate, and afterwards approached his father. And whatever his father asked him, he knew it all by heart.[35]

These quotations reveal to us the mode in which the Vedic sages speculated about the ultimate origin of all materials objects. When they perceived that on an intensely hot day people sweated or when one was internally highly excited through grief one shed tears, they could not explain its cause and took the commonest idea that appealed to their mind that heat was the cause of water. Again when they found that when it rained, the crops of all kinds grew, they concluded that water must be the cause of crops or food. This food or crop came out of the earth and therefore these were all considered as but modifications of earth, food (*anna*) is thus always used as synonymous with earth. But we find that even in this crude conception, the fire, water and earth as forming the material causes of all other things were not considered as ordinary fire, water, or earth, but as principles. These principles did not exist in their individual isolation but combined together to form all other things—even the ordinary fire, water, and earth. There is reason to believe that the doctrine of these three elements later on developed into the theories of three *guṇas* of Sāṅkhya. The three *guṇas* of Sāṅkhya are often characterised as *lohita* (red), *śukla* (white) and *kṛṣṇa* (black), and probably stand for fire, water, and earth. The doctrine that fire, water and earth combined themselves in different proportions and formed all the material objects thus represents the earliest Hindu attempt at systematically conceiving the origin of material objects as the products of the combination of three primary elements. According to this theory, air was regarded as a product of water, probably from the fact that it was found to evaporate as water vapour. In the advice of Śvetaketu's father to Śvetaketu to fast for a time in order to experience the truth of his remarks, we find the first beginnings of an experimental test of a preconceived theory.

The five elements had already been discovered in the Upaniṣads as I have already said. Thus the *Taittirīaya Upaniṣad* (ii. 1.) says: 'Truly from this *ātman* the *ākāśa* came forth; from the *ākāśa* the wind, from the wind fire, from fire water, from water the earth, from the earth the plants, from plants nourishment, from nourishment semen, from semen man.' This theory of elements must be distinguished from other mythical accounts in which the whole world is conceived as having come out of water or a golden egg.

In the Upaniṣads a primal matter, *prakṛti*, is also often alluded to, as we have already seen. When the *guṇa* theory began to be worked out by the Sāṅkhya, the *prakṛti* or primal matter referred to in the Upaniṣads was taken up by them as merely representing the earliest undisturbed state of the *guṇas*. There was still another school of thinkers who did not appreciate the theory of the *guṇas* as substantive entities; they took their stand on the doctrine of an all pervasive primal matter which showed diverse characteristics or *guṇas* (lit. quality). We have already seen how this doctrine grew and developed at the hands of the Vaiṣṇavas until we come to Veṅkaṭa. The *guṇa* doctrine, as it developed, sought to explain all phenomena excepting the soul (*puruṣa*) as being but the combinations of the *guṇa* substances. But if the intellectual phenomena had to be explained on the basis of the combinations of the *guṇas*, the *guṇa* had to be shifted beyond the borders of all manifested and unmanifested physical characters; this alone not being sufficient, one of the three *guṇas*, viz. *sattva*, was conceived as being constituted of those reals which resembled most the soul and not the other two *guṇa*-reals, the mass (*tamas*) and energy (*rajas*) with which they were always associated. In the intellectual phenomena the mass or *tamas*-reals were reduced to their ultimate minimum, whereas in the physical phenomena mass and energy prevailed and the intellectual merits of *sattva*-reals were reduced to their ultimate minimum. The conception of mass-points and energy-points as the *tamas* and *rajas*-reals were of so subtle and of potential character that they in the mselves were held as inconceivable. The Sāṅkhyists were bound to do it, for it was only in such a supra-material form that the mass and energy-reals could be associated with the *sattva*-reals. If these had any such characteristics as had any similarity with the ordinary material objects then these could hardly be considered as forming the constituents of our minds. The Sāṅkhyists therefore had to begin with their conception of matter far beyond the confines of ordinary matter. The Sāṅkhyists however held that the aggregation of these reals could produce the five infra-atomic potentials and also the atoms of five elements which combined together to form all material objects.

The Vaiśeṣikas also admitted that there were the atoms of the five elements possessing a series of gradually increasing qualities. But since the Vaiśeṣikas considered mind and its qualities as essentially different in nature from these atoms of elements, they had neither to go beyond the confines of the immediate data of matter nor to explain the evolution of these matter atoms from certain super-subtle entities as the Sāṅkhyists had to. In Sāṅkhya an atom, though a combination of the three subtle *guṇas*, was considered the smallest particle of matter, but with Vaiśeṣika the atoms were altogether partless. In their character as partless the Vaiśeṣika atoms could be compared more to the *guṇa* substances than to the atoms of Sāṅkhya. But unlike the *guṇas* these atoms were considered of five different elements. Two atoms combined together to form a *dvyaṇuka* and three *dvyaṇukas* combined together to form a *trasareṇu* and it was only as *trasareṇu* that the different elements could show their characteristic capacities. When once the mind, space and time were held as distinct entities there could be no need of offering speculations on the original evolutions of matter, these atoms of the elements were therefore regarded as eternal and not the result of any evolution. According to the Vaiśeṣika, none of the entities such as time, space and atoms of the four elements have been derived, but they all exist eternally in themselves. The Jains also did not consider that matter was the result of any evolution, holding the atoms to be eternal. They also discarded the theory of the five distinct elements which the Vaiśeṣikas and the Sāṅkhyists advocated. They held that there was only one kind of atom which possessed all the four kinds of qualities found in the four different elements—earth, air, water, fire. Such an atom has a touch property, smell property, taste property and light-heat property. These atoms combined together in different forms generally in three dimensions in different shapes and thus variety of shapes gave rise to the formation of different material objects. Democritus, we know, held that the atoms differed in size and shape and that this was responsible for the production of different material objects. But here variety of arrangement is regarded as the main reason for all differences in material objects. The Sāṅkhya also admits it, but it also believes in the existence of five different kinds of elements. The Jains thought that different kinds of atomic arrangement were alone sufficient for explaining all differences in objects; when matter was regarded as ultimate in itself, what is the use and guarantee that there were four or five different kinds of atoms? The theory of elements, we have already seen, had its basis in the Upaniṣads and naturally all Hindu systems followed it.

The Jains were outside the Hindu school of thought and they therefore proceeded in their own way and did not allow themselves to be influenced by the Hindu thought. They found that in actual experience the touch element, the taste element, the smell element and the light-heat element were never found existing separately from one another; but the same matter affected us in all the four or five kinds of sensation and therefore instead of admitting the existence of five different kinds of elements it is better to admit that the same atom presented all the five different characteristics. The Vaiśeṣika also differed from the Upaniṣadic school of thinking in this that it did not believe in the evolution of matter, but regarded the atoms of elements as eternal, whereas all other adherents of the Upaniṣadic line of thought believed in the possibility of the evolution of the elements from other subtler stages of being. It was the Buddhists, the Jains and the Vaiśeṣikas who did not believe in it and the Mīmāṃsakas, who generally followed the Nyāya-Vaiśeṣikas in these things, also agreed with the view. The Nyāya-Vaiśeṣikas admitted space also as an eternal substance which gives rise to our notions of relative space such as east, west, north and south. The Buddhist regarded *deśa* as the space only, a medium or field for the operation of the causal collocations. The Vaiṣṇavas do not admit space as the order of coexistent points; it is like time wholly relative to the understanding. It is on the basis of our ordinary experiencial consciousness in its acts of perception that there is difference between the time order and the space order, that the former can be reckoned in terms of units of moments as that which is taken up by an atom in its movement of its own dimension of space, whereas space has no unit in itself, space motion is due to the different relations in which things stand in the all-pervasive *ākāśa*. The real basis of space as all-pervasive is to be found in the extensive quantity of the *guṇas*. The grammar school often speaks of space as being a form of the mind imposed on the external world in consequence of which it appears to have an external reality. There is but one force in consequence of which the space-imagination is one, but in relation to diverse other perceptions it appears as many. Veṅkaṭa also denied the existence of *dik* or space as a separate entity.

As regards time (*kāla*) also there is the same difference of view between the Nyāya-Vaiśeṣikas, Buddhists and Jains on one side and the Sāṅkhya-Yoga, Vaiṣṇava, the grammar schools on the other. Thus with Nyāya-Vaiśeṣika *kāla* or time is a separate entity. Time is that on account of which our notions of simultaneity, succession, quickness and delay are generated. Without the admission of time as a separate entity the rise of such notions could not be justified. Thus the *Nyāyakandalī* says that our perception of things can only occur directly and immediately with reference to the objective things alone, and not time, for time is not directly perceivable. We observe changes in things as old or young and then infer that there must be some entity apart from the things which generates such notions in us. When such inference is made then things are perceived as associated with time. In our ordinary everyday experience we are not often conscious of having made such inference with regard to time, for in these cases the very sight of things bring with it its associated notion of time, just as on seeing a piece of sandal wood, even without smelling it, we say that it is fragrant. So though time cannot be directly perceived by the senses it is always inferred from such changes in things as are associated with our notions of old and new, or past and present. Though time is one, yet due to its association with diverse kinds of things it appears as many. Some astronomers such as Bhāskara also follow in general the Vaiśeṣika view and hold that since all time calculations require the association of solar revolutions and since solar revolutions cannot be directly connected with things, there must be some entity to connect them. Mādhavācārya in his *Gaṇitasārasaṃgraha* takes the unit of time measurement as that in which an atom goes beyond another atom. This unit is technically called *samaya;* a number of *samayas* make an *āvali;* a measured number of *āvalis* makes an *ucchvāsa,* seven *ucchvāsas* make one *stoka;* seven *stokas* make one *lava* and with 38 and a half of this the *ghaṭi* is formed. Two *ghaṭis* make one *muhūrtta;* thirty *muhūrttas* make one day. The Jains also believe that time (*kāla*) has a separate existence; it helps indirectly the production of changes in things. Thus Brahmadeva says that some say that *kāla* consists of the facts comprised by the rising and the setting of the sun and deny the existence of a real time. But this view is untenable, for there must be a time having the characteristics of a substance, different from the acts mentioned above. There must be something to hold these acts. *Varttana* or continuity is the perception of the existence of a substance understood from changes produced in the same in separate moment of time. For example, we put rice in a pot containing water and place the same on a fire. After some time, we find that the rice is boiled. From this it is inferred that slow changes must have been going on in the rice from the moment we put it in the raw state in the vessel till we saw it in the boiled condition. Throughout this period an existence is to be inferred. This perception of existence is called *varttana*. This inference of the existence of real time can only be made from the effects of apparent time as moments, hours, days and months. Consistently with their atomic theory the Jains consider Real Time as points, or particles which never mix with one another but are always separate. The universe is full of these particles of time, no space within it being void of the same. These particles of time are invisible, innumerable, inactive and without form; they are like so many innumerable jewels.

Patañjali in defining time (*kāla*) says in the *Mahābhāṣya* thus: That is called time by which the growth and decay of things are noticed; that entity associated with some kinds of action is called day and when associated with other kinds of action is called night. By what action? By the movement of the sun.

The Sāṅkhya-Yoga believes that time is only a creation of the understanding (*buddhi-nirmāṇa*), its smallest unit is considered to be that which is taken by an atom to move in its own dimension of space. The Vaiṣṇavas believe, like the Nyāya-Vaiśeṣika, that time is a continuous all-pervasive whole which is the cause of all changes, and, according to them, it has an identical reality with God.

From the above summary statements about the views of the different systems of Hindu philosophy we find that we can roughly divide them in four classes: (1) the empiricists, (2) the evolutionists, (3) the upholders of the commonsense view and (4) the idealists. The Sāṅkhya-Yoga and the Vaiṣṇavas may be called the evolutionists whereas the followers of the Gauḍapāda or Śaṅkara schools may be called the idealists. Among these I should also count some schools of Buddhist such as the Mādhyamikas and the Yogācāras. The grammar school of thought as represented by Patañjali in his *Mahābhāṣya*, Bhartṛhari in the *Vākyapadīya* and Helārāja in his commentary on *Vākyapadīya* may be counted as developing a commonsense philosophy with a idealistic tendency. The Nyāya, Vaiśeṣika, Mīmāṃsā, the Jains and the other schools of Buddhists may be called empiricists or realists. The evolutionists agree in the main that the ordinary objects of matter were derived from one or more fundamental substances (as in the case of Sāṅkhya-Yoga), either by stress and strain or by combination and re-combination in greater or smaller proportion. The primary substance in the school of thought has to pass through a series of evolutionary stages before reaching the ordinary state of matter. Space and time are not separate entities but are only imaginations of the understanding. It is true no doubt that Veṅkaṭa admits a separate existence of time, but that he does only in the sense that he identified time with God. Atoms as partless entities do not form any part of their doctrine for the gross matter is regarded by them as a product of the evolution of a finer substance. It is thus we find that Sāṅkhya-Yoga defines an atom as that smallest particle of matter beyond which it cannot any more be devided and Veṅkaṭa regards the particles of matter that produce the sensation of smell as the smallest particle of matter. All question of physical interest regarding the products of matter and their mutual relation as well as motion are interpreted by them in the light of evolution or modification of a primary substance either simple or composite. The schools such as Nyāya, Vaiśeṣika, the Jain, the Buddhist and the Mīmāṃsā are all realists; they all take their stand on gross matter and do not go far beyond to other categories than what is experienced by us all. The Naiyāyikas no doubt call the atoms partless, yet they believe that these all possess in an unmanifested form all the characters that are displayed by them in their gross form. The division of the elements was so permanent and steady that the Nyāya-Vaiśeṣika could not conceive that different elements could combine together. The utmost concession that they could make was this that in some classes of compounds an element was in the middle while a different element surrounded it. They were driven to this view because as they did not conceive that the different elements had a common basis, they could not conceive that they could combine together to form any compound. Later on the adherents of the Sāṅkhya-Yoga also began to be influenced by the Nyāya theory of compounds. In the theory of causation, as we shall see later on, while the Sāṅkhya-Yoga viewed all compounds as but due to the placing and replacing of the atoms which manifested gradually the new qualities held in a potential form, the Nyāya-Vaiśeṣika held that at every time new compounds and substances were formed which acquired new characteristic qualities of their own. The qualities, motion, energy, etc. are all separate and different from the substances in which they inhere. Time and space are also held as having separate independent existence. All conceptions of things are taken generally in the way in which they appear to us in our ordinary experience; they are not explained from the standpoint of a subtler basis beyond experience. Light and heat are viewed as corpuscles and all explanations of things are offered on the basis of the atomic structure. The idealists are interested in proving that all our notions of the external world are fallacious or rather illusory; time, space, matter and motion—none of these can satisfy the demands of self-consistency and are hence to be regarded as illusory. The commonsense view of grammar sought to explain the notions of things conveyed in our linguistic usages and in doing so, straining their analytic process, they reached the doctrine of cosmic energy which was at the root of all phenomena.

I do not like to compare the development of physical ideas of India with those of Greece or of those of Europe of modern times, for such comparisons are always liable to be misunderstood. I have given some of the salient points of the ideas about matter and motion among the ancient Hindus and have also given a brief sketch of the development of these ideas in Europe in ancient and modern times. The points of similarity and difference between the Indian and European viewpoints as well as the distinctive feature of the enquiries of both countries in ancient and modern times will naturally strike every impartial and thinking reader. The chief value of these speculations as it appears to me is this that they are not silly guesses but honest attempts at understanding problems with which the ancient sages of India were confronted; the facts at their disposal were but few, but their speculations were rather deep; any and every philosopher did not give his own view at random, but there were different schools of speculation and there were different systems in which speculations about the exterior world proceeded. The object of the speculators was not the scientific interest of solving the problems of the physical world or of finding out means and ways for adapting any knowledge about them for the utility of mankind or merely to give a rational explanation of the world but it was only for the sake of understanding the true destiny and relations of the souls of ourselves as moral and religious persons that the Hindu sages ought to solve any difficult problem about the world that confronted them. But when they were confronted with such problems they did not evade them, but tried their best mainly on the strength of a prior reason to explain the facts of physical experience as presented to them. Their explanations about the physical world were always formed in strict consistency with their other view of metaphysics. The truths they arrived at were the results of systematic reasonings which tried to refute other theories on the subject and establish their own. Their limitations when compared to what we have in modern times are mainly due to the extreme paucity of facts that were known to them. But it is interesting to note that generally the way of thinking that they followed had great similarity so far as bare outlines are concerned with many of the attempts that have been made in Europe up to the modern times.

PART TWO

Theories of Cosmic Changes

The growth of the Smṛti literature of the 14th and the 15th centuries with its artificial, stringent, and unmeaning laws of society and religion, are so much associated with the dead and inert life of the few generations of the past and even of the majority of the people of the recent generation that it is indeed difficult even for an Indian to have a distinct view of its past history and culture. When we look at the dogmatic grip of the scripture over the popular mind and the slavish admiration and veneration of the people for them, even when the march of time and progress has forced them to break most of such laws, or vision is dimmed and blurred, an honest doubt creeps into our mind, whether we really possessed any true life or whether boasted antiquity was as lifeless as the rocky walls of the Himalayas which have stood the test of time since the beginning of the world. With the light of the present generation as far as we can see, we find only sandy shoals, obstructing the free flow of the current of life which has been undermining our physical, intellectual and spiritual vitality. We look at the spontaneity of the western world, and seriously ask ourselves, did we even seek truth for its own sake? Had we ever the courage of our own convictions, did we ever follow straight in the path dictated by reasons? Had we ever true freedom and sincerity of thoughts and speech or, in brief, had we ever Life?

It is indeed difficult to answer these questions, for the popular pseudo-patriotic convictions which exalt at the sight of an aeroplane as being the revival of the *puṣpaka ratha* of the *Purāṇas* are not only useless but insulting and ludicrous. One has to be sceptical like Descartes and to dive deep into the past Sanskrit literature with an honest enquiry after truth. Such a course reveals to us the true place of our forefathers and instead of readymade laws of the Smṛtis, the omniscience and the omnipotence of the *munis* or sages, we discover human beings with their doubts and ignorances, men engaged in the honest endeavour of seeking after truth steering in an ocean of darkness amidst countless failures breaking upon them. It is just when we come here that we feel that we are moving among men and not among the mummies and curios of an old museum.

In the earliest stages of the Vedas people were indeed much more easy-going and their imaginations were simple and childlike, for it was just the dawning period of human intellect. It was through the pleasure of Indra that the rains poured down from the heavens, the lightning stroke was his terrible *vajra* (thunder). Varuṇa brought about the night. It was the daily Uṣas who led men to work. Everything had its simple cause in the deities presiding over them. Thus we see that the people of the Vedic period were hardly aware of the immense complexity of the problems before them. When they stood before the mighty forces of nature they were filled with awe and fear for the supposed beings who ruled over them and naturally sought to satisfy them with hymns and oblations. They had not the courage to question the power and authority of these gods. Their intellects were in their infancy and generations after generations began to inherit the belief of their forefathers without the slightest question or doubt being raised. But even in this infant period of civilisation we meet with free minds who could raise up their heads amongst the multitudes of the fraternity and say:

> Nor aught nor naught existed, yon bright sky was not, nor Heaven's broad roof outstretched above. What covered all? What sheltered? What concealed? Was it the water's fathomless abyss? There was not death, hence there was not immortal, There was no confine between day and night, The Only One breathed breathless in himself, other than it there nothing since has been. Darkness there was and all at first was veiled in gloom profound, an ocean without light. The germ that all lay covered in the husk burst forth, one nature, from the fervent heat. Then first came love upon it, the new spring of mind—yea, poets in their hearts discerned, pondering, this bond between created things and uncreated comes this apart from earth, piercing and all-pervading, or from Heaven? The seeds were sown and mighty power arose nature below and power and will above. Who knows the secret? Who proclaim

it here? Whence, whence this manifold creation spring? The gods themselves came later into being—who knows from whence this great creation sprang. Whether his will created or was mute, the most High seer that is in highest Heaven, He knows it—or perchance even He knows not.

It is interesting to compare this agnostic conviction with the *Puruṣa-sūkta* which declares that Brahmins came from the mouth of the *Puruṣa*, the Kṣatriyas from the hand, the Vaiśyas from the things and the Śūdras from the legs. As it is out of place here, we cannot go into details to make a sifting examination of other *sūktas* of a similar attempt; but for the purpose of an illustration I believe only this *sūkta* is enough to show that even in the Vedic period amongst the host of simple believers there was gradually springing up free thinkers who had the courage of their convictions to utter an agnostic faith, to throw doubts even on such vital points of religion and faith as to shake their very foundation: 'Whether there was ever a creation or not.'

The next important epoch of Indian thought is the period of the Upaniṣads. The characteristic tendency of this period is its search for the truth. They knew that the face of truth was hidden with a golden cup. But they had sincerely engaged themselves is the task of opening it. In the *Chāndogya* and the *Bṛhadāraṇyaka*, we find how a number of sages went from place to place in search of teachers who could teach them the nature of truth, how they failed in many places and how regardless they were in this quest of truth of any social or any other kinds of restrictions until they could get a satisfactory answer. They did not care whether the teacher was a Brahmin or a Kṣatriya. In this sincere quest they have themselves recorded many of their failures, the stages through which they passed in their solution of the deep problems of reality. But though the solution which they had arrived at were the most luminous for the time (to say the least), yet in their sincere spirit of enquiry the belief often forced upon themselves that the ultimate mysteries of the world were unknowable and that 'those who think that they have known are really the most ignorant, whereas they who think that the Truth cannot be known are really the wisest. It is this consciousness and awakening that is real immortal knowledge.'

In the development of their agnosticism some of them even questioned the value of knowledge and said: 'They who are for Nescience enter into the blinding darkness, but those who are engaged in the pursuit of knowledge enter into still more blinding darkness' (*Īśā*, 9). Ignorance is bad but knowledge is worse. We do not of course know with what spirit they said it, but it is most probable that they thought that our knowledge was most vain when it dared to gauge the depth of true reality.

The whole history of this Upaniṣadic era is the record of the unaided human mind to conceive the underlying reality—reality behind the manifold of appearance, the permanent behind the changeable. There is the struggle of mind, there are fantastic and grotesque fancies and failures and there are the most brilliant successes. But whatever there might be here is the flow of life and the free movement of the human mind to grasp some of the eternal problems of the mysteries of the world. Whatever might be spoken of this period of Hindu culture it cannot be said that there was any system in the thoughts of the sages of this time. There is no doubt that they often uttered eternal truths of the highest value, but these were mere occasional glimpses and visions or side revelations of truths, the result of their abstract speculations, but not the product of any systematic and logical researches. Such a period first foreshadows the foundation of the schools of Hindu philosophy.

These schools of philosophy originated when the different speculations of the Upaniṣadic period began to take definite shape and were being gradually distinguished from one another and began to attract separate groups of adherents. These thinkers probably started with some of their favourite Upaniṣadic tenets which were in themselves crude and abstract. Consecrating themselves to particular lines of thinking with some of the conceptions of the Upaniṣads as their motto, they were confronted with diverse problems of world, god and soul, which did not so clearly appear to the simple minds of the sages of the Upaniṣads.

Thus starting with the speculations of the Upaniṣads as their groundwork diverse schools of thought began to grow in their endeavour to work out independently the different concrete problems which roused their thoughts, anticipated one another's arguments for and against particular views and tried to meet them according to the system of their own thought. Thus it is very probable that long before these speculations were recorded in the form of aphorism the separate schools of Hindu philosophy were simultaneously and independently growing in an atmosphere of rivalry amongst one another. It is important to note in this connection that in addition to the rivalry amongst the different orthodox systems there were also the heterodox systems, namely, the Cārvāka, the Bauddha, and the Jaina systems, which contributed to some of the essential features of their development.

To trace the idea of evolution from the time of the Upaniṣads, we find it stated in the *Chāndogya Upaniṣad* that originally all these manifold things were in an unmanifested condition and it was from this unmanifested Being that everything developed. From its desire to become many Fire was produced, from the desire of this Fire to become many Water was produced, from the desire of this Water to become many Earth was produced. It is from these three that everything was produced. It is by the union or combination of these three principles through the agency of an all-pervading life-principle that even ordinary fire etc. were produced. Indeed all the objects of the world are the productions of their combination. But through all things of the world, intelligent as well as the unintelligent, pervades the *prāṇa* or life, the great Brahman, and He is the source of all power.

All that can be made of this is that this manifold world had been manifested from a life-principle, the Brahman, and all force, all power, all life, have emanated from it. Quite opposite to it are the Cārvāka schools which do not regard life, *prāṇa*, or anything of the sort as any separate principle. In these Nihilists, no trace of whose works can now be found, we have a band of free thinkers who had the courage to give a bold expression of their revolutionary views as a protest against the orthodox schools. All that we can know of them now is from the references to them the orthodox systems of philosophy had to make in refuting their views. These Nihilists regarded all ritualism as vain and also inferences had no value with them, as they were always based on inductive generalisation which had no certainty. Perception with them was the only source of knowledge. They did not believe that man had any soul but regarded all life as combination of matter which manifested itself under conditions of particular combinations. This Lokāyata or popular view did not offer any theory about the evolution of the world, as such a thing could not be developed without the aid of inference which according to them had no ultimate validity.

The other strong heterodox system which did not admit the existence of any permanent soul was that of the Buddhist. According to their theory also the eternal dynamics of action conglomerated the different classes of atoms and in particular cases of such combinations life shone forth as the product. There were two classes of such combinations, the mental called *cittaka*, and the physical, called *bhautika*; the mental conglomeration of the five groups, *rūpa* (perception), *vedanā*, (feeling) *vijñāna* (consciousness), *saṃjñā* (name) and *saṃskāra* (association). The conglomerations (*saṅghāta*) of these five clusters formed the psychical plane of man, whereas the atoms of the five *bhūtas* formed the basis of the physical plane in man, animals, the vegetable and the inorganic world. There is no consciousness or life apart from these conglomerations in the background. The conglomerations are in themselves more or less of a mechanical nature, brought about neither by such a conscious principle as soul nor by an omnipotent God, but by the dynamics of eternal chains of causes and effects. Each particular being—inorganic, vegetable or the animal—is determined by the particular nature of the conglomeration that is brought about. There is no ruler either in man or in nature save the force of action. In all such conglomeration each of the elements entering into it performs its own functions. The order of the world is to be found in the regulative world order of the forces of actions. Thus is explained the manifold reality of the material world, by the forces of dying conglomerations on the atoms of matter which break them up and then unite them up in a diverse fashion. Therefore, the universe is undergoing change at every moment; there is no stability anywhere, but change. This change in the material world is brought about by the atomic changes which are continually taking place in the body of every conglomeration. It is therefore that no conglomeration can be the same at any two moments. They are breaking up at every moment and fresh conglomerations are being formed by the very force of the dying or breaking up of the old forms. All this breaking up and fresh formation is the result of the collocation of atoms and the eternal potent energy associated with them, which becomes kinetic at each stage of the progressive march of the conglomeration. This is their doctrine called *paticca-samuppāda.*

Of the orthodox systems of philosophy, the Kāpila and the Pātañjala Sāṅkhya, and Kaṇāda's system of Vaiśeṣika seem to be most notable in their speculations on the material world. The idealistic system of the Vedānta concentrates its attention on metaphysical side, the noumenon rather than the physical side or the phenomenon. The noumenon as opposed to the phenomenon, the permanent behind the changing, the stable behind the unstable engrosses all their attention. They do not indeed ignore the claims of the appearances all around us, but divert all our attention to the permanent and the real as its background. It is therefore that their speculation is generally silent about the material aspect of the world and it is only in the later period that we find that some of them borrow the tenets of the Sāṅkhya system in explaining the material world, in giving us an account of the world of appearance.

Of the other systems, the two schools of Sāṅkhya and Kaṇāda's system of Vaiśeṣika, the achievements of the former are by far the more remarkable as will appear from our explanation later on. The difference between the adherents of a system of philosophy in Europe and in India is this that all the philosophical systems in this country started with the avowed purpose of obtaining true knowledge by which a man could attain salvation and be released from the pains and troubles of this world. The people therefore who flocked round any teacher of a particular system did not do it either from pedantry, curiosity, or even for the sake of acquiring knowledge for its own sake, but from an intense desire of obtaining salvation through the acquiring of true knowledge. It is therefore that we find that the teachers of each and every school of philosophy had been continuing to impart this firm instruction from generations to generations even to the present day. Whenever any thinker emerged from amongst the adherents of any particular school, he did not attempt to distinguish himself by writing original works but generally wrote commentaries following the footprints of his past teachers, whose teachings had been handed over to him through an unbroken chain of traditions of hundreds of years and used all their intellects in interpreting the views of these old teachers. Whenever he had any original idea to communicate he generally assigned a subordinate and humble position to himself. It is therefore that we find that whereas in Europe any system of philosophy even of modern date, such as those of Kant and Hegel, exists only in printed works and are taught in colleges to pupils who would hardly think of taking any one of them as their master, here in India even now there are hundreds of disciples who are receiving instructions from the ascetics of the Vedānta or the Sāṅkhya schools which were founded probably twenty or twenty-five centuries ago. Ravages of time, political misfortunes, jealousies of rival schools, changes of economic conditions of the country had often destroyed works extending over many centuries, but even then the traditions were not altogether lost, being passed over from mouth to mouth in an unbroken chain of teachers and pupils and later incorporated in commentaries of much recent date. Thus, for example, the Sāṅkhya system of philosophy was possibly the oldest system of thought; the *Artha-śāstra* of Kauṭilya makes a mention of it, the *Śrīmadbhagavadgītā* speaks of it and references to it are found in the *Mahābhārata* and other ancient works. So far as we know from the references made to it in other systems and in the extant works of the system itself, we find that it had probably many important works. Even in Śaṅkara's time it was probably one of the most dominant systems containing a huge literature with many commentaris. But most of these works are now lost, and those that remain, excepting the *Kārikā* of Īśvarakṛṣṇa, are of comparatively recent date. The commentaries of the Pātañjala school of Sāṅkhya with the exception of the *Vyāsa-bhāṣya* are not older than the 9th century. An enquirer willing to give an account of the two schools of the old Sāṅkhya doctrine therefore can hardly ignore the Sāṅkhya literature of commentaries beginning from the 9th century. But in doing this he has the least chance of apprehending that the doctrines which he is picking up from this later period do not represent the old doctrines; for the old doctrines being regarded with the highest veneration and sacredness by their disciples were being handed over without the least alteration. Thus it is that the hymns of the Vedas, though they had long remained in the mouths of the reciters, have come down to us with the most insignificant variation. It is therefore that a through mastery over the great literature of commentaries beginning with Śaṅkarācārya or Kumārila of the 8th century is indispensably necessary for a correct interpretation of the orthodox systems which were founded at least 1000 years before that. In giving an account of the course of material evolution of the ancient Hindus, I have therefore found it necessary to incorporate the traditional accounts as preserved in the commentaries of the later centuries.

Beginning with the orthodox schools, the systems which immediately attract our attention are the Nyāya-Vaiśeṣika theories of Gautama and Kaṇāda. Unlike the Buddhist, the Vedāntist and the Sânkhyist they did not regard that *ākāśa* had any atomic structure; *ākāśa*, with them, was the mere inert substratum for the propagation of sound waves. The atoms of the same class again unite, according to them, by two to form molecules called *dvyaṇukas* with the exception of the still atmospheric air which is only the accumulated mass of loose atoms. The atoms are always vibratory. Now these molecules of the same *bhūta* containing two atoms again combine by twos, threes, or fours to form further aggregates. According to this view, the molecules of any *bhūta* could not contain more than two atoms. But there was another view, as we find it from the accounts of Utpala in his commentary on *Bṛhat-saṃhitā*, that two, three, or four atoms were admitted to unite together by their natural vibratory motion to form molecules. So long as there is no action of heat, these molecules of the different *bhūtas* show only their homogeneous characters. But by the actions of heat these molecules of the different *bhūtas* are diversely arranged and collocated and it is on account of this diversity of collocations that the different genera and species are formed. Molecules of the atoms from the same *bhūta* even, say *kṣiti*, may arrange and rearrange themselves in diverse ways by the action of heat and form thousands of different substances. The factors which operate in the formation of these different substances are: (1) the density of the grouping (*vyūha*), (2) the position of the atoms or molecules in the separate rearrangements forming different substances (*avayava-sannivesa*), (3) the different kinds of *pāka* or heat associated with them in the making of the different rearrangements. Thus Śrīdhara says: Even though there may not be any diversity in the atoms of any *bhūta*, these, propelled by the Unseen (Moral Destiny), may so arrange themselves that different species of substance might be manifested. Uddyotakara also says: There is no differentiation of species in the atoms themselves.

Śrīdhara further says that there is no ultimate difference between the atoms of a barley seed and the paddy seed, or between the atoms of the semen and ovum, as they are all but modifications of earth. Uddyotakara again says: Heat is not the only cause which sets the change of such character as colour etc., but the diversity of the change also depends upon the previous nature of the substance. The changes produced by heat upon a body suffering under the thermal influence is conditioned by its previous characters according to which the heat generates further new changes of colour etc. Vācaspati also says: Though according to our theory there is no difference in the molecules forming the matter of substance, yet owing to the diverse nature of the distinction of the different previous characters of bodies there arise different kinds of smell, colour, taste and touch and the different species are generated depending on the diversity of the nature of heat. *Nyāyabodhinī*, the commentary on Annam Bhaṭṭa's *Tarkasaṃgraha*, writes: Heat is of different kinds. The one which generates colour is different from that which generates taste. So also in the case of touch. Thus owing to the diversity of effects we have to assume diversity of the nature of heat. When a cow eats grass, the grass matter being broken up into atoms and by the action of some particular kind of heat, the old colour, taste, touch and smell, being destroyed, there comes in another kind of heat which generates those kinds of colour etc. found in milk; and now the atoms possessed of those new kinds of colour etc. generate a binary molecule and by the aggregation of these gross milk is formed.

Whenever they speak of heat, they speak of it as an entity which reminds us of the corpuscular theory. It penetrates into the interatomic spaces in cases of transparency, it vibrates, rises up and goes down and moves in any rectilinear direction. It is by the action of this heat that substances are broken up into the atomic or molecular stages and are again re-united in fresh rearrangement.

It may not be out of place here to note an important contribution of the Jains in this connection. According to them, mere juxtaposition by heat of atoms was not sufficient for their combination. The atoms which are to combine must possess two peculiar opposite characters. When both the atoms possess positive or negative characters, generally they cannot attract each other and there is no combination. When the opposed qualities are equal in intensity, then also there is no combination. In certain cases when one of the atoms is possessed of very strong character (double or more) and the other with a very feeble one, then even the similar ones may be attracted by one another. It is this attraction which constitutes the bond of unity without which mere juxtaposition is not sufficient to unite any two atoms. Thus we find in *Tattvārthādhigama*: 'Is juxtaposition sufficient to bring about a combination or is there any other condition? When there is juxtaposition then an atom having a bond is united. The bond is due to smoothness and roughness but not when the qualities are very feeble. The bond takes place when there is juxtaposition between the smooth and the rough; very feeble smooth and very feeble rough do not combine. It has been said by you that when the character is not very feeble then the smooth and the rough have a bond. But can those which possess similar characters never combine? Not only similar qualities, when they are equal in power. Atoms possessing similar characters or qualities of equal force possess no bond. Thus a smooth one cannot combine with another one having the same smoothness. So also with the rough. What is the condition of the combination of those which possess qualities of same force? Those with similar forces have a bond only when they have different characters. Are the opposite characters of similar force combined unconditionally? Those having the same force are combined only when their qualities are double or more powerful: double or more powerful smooth with smooth, double or more powerful rough with rough.'

Passing over again to our original Nyāya-Vaiśeṣika position as contrasted to the Jaina position just stated, we find that combination here is possible only among the atoms of the same element, or among the different modifications of the same *bhūta*. It is only in some limited cases where the atoms of the same *bhūta* do not combine under the action of heat that these require to be surrounded by the atoms of other *bhūta*. Thus, for example, in the case of fruit juice or oils, the earth atoms must be dissolved in water and it is when the water atoms surround the earth atoms that some new forces are set up and under the influence of heat the earth atoms assume new characters (colour, taste, etc.). In all such cases the water atoms excite the earth atom. Here the water atom is the instrument through which the earth atom assumes new characters. Similarly, other atoms of *vāyu*, or *tejas* may also act in a similar way and earth particles may also act in a similar way with regard to the atoms of other *bhūtas*. This phenomenon is known in Sanskrit as *upaṣṭambhana*.

With the exception of these, most cases of the general and the species are due to the rearrangement of the atoms of the same *bhūta*. All changes whatsoever are due to this re-arrangement. This grouping is the only cause of all changes whatsoever.

Now there is another question over which the Vaiśeṣikas and the Naiyāyikas hold divergent views. The question is when any gross substance is changed by the influence of heat in such a way as to possess diverse qualities of colour, taste, touch, etc., i.e. when it is changed into some other substance, how does the change begin? Is the substance first decomposed into atoms and by their different re-grouping form the new substance, or is it that the process of decomposition proceeds up to the molecules and then these molecules re-group themselves to form new substances? The former view is held by the Vaiśeṣika school of Kaṇāda, by virtue of which they are called Pīlupāka-vādins; and the latter school of Gautama holds the molecular view and they are called Piṭharapāka-vādins.

Now after this brief survey of the Nyāya-Vaiśeṣika view, we see that all the objective world of matter are generally formed by the various kinds of grouping of the spherical atoms of the same *bhūta* or the groupings of the atoms of the modifications of the same *bhūta* entering into the compound for the formation of the fresh substance, and sometimes among the atoms of the different *bhūtas* when one of them acts as the surrounding dynamic.

The atoms were conceived to be spherical in shape but it was something like a point without any dimensions; and it is by the groupings of these that the whole universe is formed.

It appears, there is seemingly no difference between this view and the Sāṅkhya view which we shall describe later so far as the constitution of matter is concerned. But the difference lies in this that in this view no new character can arise which is not already existent in the atoms and there is no evolution of new qualities out of the inherent dynamics of the substance as in the Sāṅkhya system. In that system, as we shall see later, a new substance may arise by spontaneous self-grouping of the atoms without the interference of any external action. New qualities like new substances are only readjustments of the old and continual changes are going on by spontaneous disintegration and recombination. But in the Nyāya-Vaiśeṣika system there can never be any change of substance or quality without the action of one component upon another: and any molecule cannot have any quality which is not possessed by each of its component atoms. The character of any atom cannot manifest itself until it can link itself with other atoms of its own class. The whole world is explained on a basis of chemical synthesis and all things are looked at from a detached point of view rather than from the point of view of conservation of energy. Life itself is the product of diverse chemical synthesis. All action of matter on matter is reduced to motion with the exception of conscious activity. The combination of the atoms to form diverse substances and 'controller in the background in the shape of the unseen moral destiny,' which in its turn was presided over by God. The atoms themselves were never created. There is no separate entity or force apart from the modes of motion. The effect is in all cases the resultant of the combined motion of the various causes involved (*kāraka-cakra*).

Most of these theories about the material world of the ancient Hindus were probably based upon the observation of nature and abstract speculation. Experiments were also performed with regard to metallurgy, dyeing, pharmacy, surgery, etc. But experiments as scientific methods of discovery, I believe, they had very little. The elaborate system of Hindu medicine, their fair knowledge of the anatomy of the human body show that they must have been experimenting from a long time past and for long periods before they could come to such definite and concrete knowledge of things where speculation could not have been of much use. But it is indeed very regrettable that that atmosphere of acquiring concrete knowledge by combining speculation with experiments soon vanished for reasons which cannot now be definitely ascertained. It might be political, economical, social or all of them combined. In going through Caraka we also find that very often great assemblies were held of learned men who discussed the separate aspects of diverse problems and compared their own independent observations with one another. But whatsoever these might have been we must admit that abstract logical speculations of bold minds seems to have produced all that we may find often in the ancient Hindu literature. The value of these in modern times lies first in the interest that men of all ages should necessarily feel, in the early struggles of the unaided human mind, groping in the dark and getting occasional glimpses of light in their sincere quest after truth. Secondly, it also shows how much pure speculation and abstract thinking can do in discovering truths of the material world. Though definite and concrete knowledge in these matters cannot be gained without the help of well-regulated experiments, yet it cannot be denied that by studying them we can often get the most valuable suggestions which may sometimes have even a great practical value.

Proceeding further in our search after the most prominent ideas about the material world and its evolution from the material point of view, the system that fully engrosses our attention is that of the two schools of Sāṅkhya—of Kapila and Patañjali. The Vedāntists engrossed as they were with their idealism were but poor thinkers about the material world. The early Vedāntist had therefore but little to say with their Trivṛtkaraṇa and Pañcīkaraṇa of any great importance and do not deserve attention in a brief survey like this. The Vedāntists of later times are often found, as we have stated before, appropriating the Sāṅkhya ideas of the material world and grafting their metaphysical speculations on them. We should now therefore begin with the idea of evolution and the conceptions that the Sāṅkhyists had of it and their achievements in the matter together with the achievements of the medical schools of Caraka and Suśruta who had followed the doctrines of the Sāṅkhyists in explaining the process of evolution.

From the Sāṅkhya point of view, evolution may be described in the words of Dr. B.N. Seal in its formal aspect as the 'differentiation in the integrated (*saṃsṛṣṭa-viveka*). In other words, the process of evolution consists in the development of the differentiated (*vaiṣamya*) within the undifferentiated (*sāmyāvasthā*), of the determinate (*viśeṣa*) within the indeterminate (*aviśeṣa*), of the coherent (*yutasiddha*), within the incoherent (*ayutasiddha*). The evolutionary series is subject to a definite law which it cannot overstep (*pariṇāma-krama-niyama*). The order of succession is not from whole to parts, nor from parts to whole, but ever from a relatively less differentiated, less determinate, less coherent whole to a relatively more differentiated, more determinate, more coherent whole. That the process of differentiation evolves out of homogeneity separate or unrelated parts, which are then integrated into a whole, and that this whole again breaks up by fresh differentiation into isolated factors for a subsequent reintegration and so on *ad infinitum* is a fundamental misconception of the *course of material evolution*. That the antithesis stands over against a thesis, and that the synthesis supervenes and imposes unity *ab extra* on these two independent and mutually hostile moments, is the same radical misconception as regards *the dialectical form* of cosmic development. On the Sānkhya view, increasing differentiation proceeds *pari passu* with increasing integration within the evolving whole, so that by this twofold process what was an incoherent indeterminate homogeneous whole evolves into a coherent determinate heterogeneous whole.'[36]

According to this Pariṇāma theory, the supermental, mental, and extra-mental series of effects have all taken place by the varying collocations of the three reals—*sattva*, *rajas* and *tamas*.

The *manas* and the senses, which I have rendered as the 'Mental' have been generated by the collocations of the *guṇas* in which *sattva* and *rajas* have predominated in various proportions over the *tamas*, the effects of which have become extremely minimised in all the functions of all the ten senses and their superintendent, the *manas*.

The extra-mental series or the physical world of matter and motion is the result of a series of collocations of the *guṇas* in which the *sattva* had been extremely subordinated to the absolute preponderance of *tamas*, the mass, and *rajas*, the energy.

Gross matter is composed of the five kinds of *bhūtas*—*ākāśa*, *tejas*, *vāyū*, *ap* and *kṣiti*. These atoms of the five gross *bhūtas* are in their turn generated from the five finer and subtler atoms, called the *tanmātras*, of *ākāśa*, *tejas*, *vāyu*, *ap* and *kṣiti* by the gradual accretion of mass or materiality and by peculiar mutual combination. Thus in the words of Dr. B.N. Seal 'If we take a unit of rudiment matter (*bhūtādi*) of the unit of mass (cf. the mass of an electron with a charge of motion etc.) and represent the first *tanmātra* by t_1 such units, and if further t_2, t_3, t_4, t_5 units of mass (*bhūtādi*) be successively added at each accretion to form a fresh *tanmātra,* then the 2nd, 3rd, 4th and 5th *tanmātras* will respectively contain t_1+t_2, $t_1+t_2+t_3$, $t_1+t_2+t_3+t_4$ and $t_1+t_2+t_3+t_4+t_5$ units of mass.

'Also the *vāyu* atom (bi-*tanmātric* system) will contain $t_1+(t_1+t_2)$, i.e. $2t_1+t_2$ units of mass; the *tejas* atom (tri-*tanmātric* system) will contain $t_1+(t_1+t_2)+(t_1+t_2+t_3)$, i.e. $3t_1+2t_2+t_3$ units; the Ap atom (tetra-tanmātric system) $t_1+(t_1+t_2)+(t_1+t_2+t_3)+(t_1+t_2+t_3+t_4)$, i.e. $4t_1+3t_2+2t_3+t_4$ units....'[37]

The illustrative qualities of the five *bhūtas* have been described by Vācaspati Miśra as follows:

The characteristics of *pṛthivī* are inertia, heaviness, roughness, destruction, stability, manifestation, difference, support, turbidity, hardness, enjoyability.

Of *Ap*: smoothness, subtlety, clearness, whiteness, softness, heaviness, coolness, preservation, purity, combination.

Of *Tejas*: going upward, cooking, burning, lightness, shining, destruction, power.

Of *Vāyu*: transverse motion, purification, throwing, pushing, strength, movability, throwing no shadow, roughness.

Of *Ākāśa*: motion in all directions, non-agglomeration and non-obstruction.

The *ākāśa* is described by Caraka as that medium which offers no resistance. He further writes that the qualities of the five *bhūtas* can be grasped by the cognitive sense. He adds that the actual properties of the *bhūtas* are undefinable. They exist in the *bhūtas* themselves, the characteristic qualities described are only signs by which we can differentiate them from one another, the qualities or properties assigned to them only represent the ways and modes in which the different *bhūtas* can affect our five cognitive senses. It is therefore that the characteristic qualities of the five *bhūtas* are often found to be differently enumerated from different points of view. Thus Caraka describes them as follows: The earth, water, air and fire possess roughness, liquidity, movement and heat. Suśruta characterises *kṣiti* and *ap* from two points of view—static and dynamic: *kṣiti* possesses two different types of qualities, viz. compactness, steadiness, roughness, heaviness, hardness, smell and pungent taste on one side and the power of producing accumulation, conglomeration and also the downward movement on the other. *Ap*, the water principle, possesses cold, steadiness, smoothness, movability, slowness, slight pungent sour taste on one side and the power of making smooth, cheering up, oozing, etc. on the other.

We thus see that the representation of the physical world as being made up of the atoms of the five *bhūtas* is based on the fact that our senses are being affected by the external world in five different ways. From the characteristic difference of the affectation of our senses the Sāṅkhyists have inferred the characteristic differences in the atomic composition or the structure of the *bhūtas* as we have previously said, while showing the Mono-tanmātric, bi-*tanmātric*, tri-*tanmātric*, tetra-*tanmātric*, and the penta-*tanmātric* composition of the atoms of the five *bhūtas* beginning in an ascending order from *ākāśa*.

In the constitution of the *tanmātras* we find that the *vāyu*, *tejas*, *ap*, and *kṣiti tanmātras* are all developed from *ākāśa tanmātra*, simply with the accretion of a fresh unit of mass and consequent fresh distribution of and re-distribution of the principle of energy, *rajas*, at every stage of development. It is therefore that we find that the most developed *kṣiti tanmātra* contains all that was contained in the *ākāśa*, *tejas*, *vāyu*, and *ap tanmātras*, but owing to the accretion of a fresh unit of mass and consequent fresh distribution and re-distribution of energy in order to assimilate the fresh accretion of mass appears as more developed or grosser than the other *tanmātras*.

In the development of the atoms of the five *bhūtas* from the *tanmātras* we find that here also there is fresh accretion of units of mass at every step. But the peculiarity lies in this that all the *tanmātras* of the subtler *bhūtas* take part in the formation of the atoms of the corresponding grosser *bhūtas*. Accretion of mass is no doubt made at every step, but these accretions are made to the *tanmātras* themselves as we have already explained in a symbolical way. Thus we see that from one unit of mass charged with energy or *rajas* gradually with the accretion of mass and consequent distribution and re-distribution of energy the *tanmātras* have evolved and from them again with further accretion of mass and action of energy the *bhūtas* have evolved. The later stages of the evolutionary process not only preserve all that was contained in the preceding stages but grow richer in qualities. Thus the qualities of *ākāśa* are seen to exist in *vāyu* which in addition to that develops another quality of *sparśa* of *vāyu* and in addition to them *rūpa*; so again *ap* contains in addition to *śabda, sparśa* and *rūpa* of *tejas, rasa;* and so on.

After the formation of the atoms of the *bhūtas* further combinations also take place owing to the diverse arrangements of the atoms of a *bhūta* through *rajas* or Energy. Thus we see that in annotating upon Suśruta text on 'Gold Silver Gems Jewels Earth and others' Dalhaṇa writes: By the word 'others' iron-ore, sand, lime, arsenic, etc., are to be taken.

Thus we find that gold, silver, crystal, magnet, red arsenic, earth, ore, silicon, lime, sulphurret of arsenic are called to be the modifications of the element known as *kṣiti.* Now we have seen that each of the atoms of *kṣiti, ap, tejas,* etc. represent a group or a system of *tanmātras.* In these systems of *tanmātras*, the *tanmātra* which represents the special character of the *bhūta* remains supreme though the other *tanmātras* of a lower state of development are also present in the system of *tanmātras* forming the constitution of the atom, only in a subordinate way. Thus Vācaspati writes: The earthy atom is born from the five classes of ultimate atoms (*tanmātras*) with a prevalence of the odoriferous minima. So also the liquid atom of *ap* is born from the four classes of ultimate atoms except the odoriferous minima with a prevalence of the gustiferous minima. Similarly the fiery atom is made of the three minima besides the odoriferous and the gestiferous minima, of the tangeferous and soniferous and the luminiferous minima, with a predominance of the latter. Similarly the gaseous atom is born from the tangeferous and soniferous minima without any admixture of the other three classes of minima with a prevalence of the tangeferous minima. Similarly the birth of *ākāśa* is from the one class of soniferous minima atom.

The system of *tanmātras* forming the constitution of the atom of the *bhūta* being unchangeable, the cause of the difference in composition of different substances as modifications of particular *bhūtas* must be sought in the difference in the collocation and arrangements and re-arrangements of the atoms of that particular *bhūta*.

We see however that substances are made of the combination of two or more *bhūtas* together. In such cases however the atoms of different kinds of the *bhūtas* stand side by side with one another. Thus when we look at penta-*bhautic* object the atoms of smell, taste and touch remain side by side with the *tejas* atoms. These atoms—all being side by side in very close succession—it becomes impossible for us to notice the gap between one atom and another. All things in the physical world of ours are composed of the atoms of the five *bhūtas*. The atoms are always vibrating by the energy of *rajas* with which they are charged and this vibration of atoms is the cause of changes of all kinds in nature. Thus in one moment of time, as the atoms of all things are vibrating and changing their respective positions, the whole world is undergoing a change or evolution. The physical movement of the atoms in *ākāśa*, space or ether, there is thus the cause of all kinds of changes whether they be chemical, physical, or of any other kind. Chemical and physical changes differ in degree, but not in kind, for change can happen in one way only, namely, the changes of the atoms of their respective places. It is on account of this change that things are generated; that these can grow and then again suffer decay and die and other things are generated. All birth, growth and decay of any kind results from this continual ceaseless movement of the atoms in *ākāśa* or ether.

It is theoretically possible to change anything in the world to any other thing, provided the necessary changes in the collocation of the atoms could be arranged.

There is no intrinsic difference between one thing and another save that the position or manner in which the atoms are arranged in one substance differ from the position of the atoms in another.

The unevolved form exist always in a latent form in the evolved modifications of substances. The change or modification only gives expressions to the latent varieties of the substances. As the atoms change their position by their innate *rajas* or energy, the substance changes its form and manifests diverse new qualities which could not be perceived before. The atoms however are ceaselessly vibrating and changing their positions and consequent undergoing change. At first the changes being insignificant are imperceptible but gradually with cumulation these become remarkable and then only we can detect the changes undergone by the substance.

But though, theoretically speaking, everything is the cause of every other thing, yet the course of changes follows a definite law which it cannot overstep and this is what is meant by *pariṇāma-krama-niyama*.

In this way the vegetable kingdom passes into the animal kingdom and that again is reduced into vegetable and *ap* together with earth accretions transforms itself into the thousand different kinds of juices.

'The variety of all forms of juices etc. due to the changes of earth and water is seen in stationery objects. So also of the stationary in the self moving, and of the self moving in the stationery. Thus all is of the nature of all without the destruction of the species.' (*Vyāsa-bhāṣya*)

'The liquid is possessed of the soneferous, tangeferous, luminiferous, and gestiferous atoms. The earth is possessed of the soneferous, tangeferous, luminiferous, the gestiferous, and the odoriferous atoms. A modification of all these is seen in the variety of all the forms of juice etc. found in the roots, fruits, flowers and leaves. All these cannot be the modifications of either the solid or the liquids different in nature from themselves. It has of course been shown that nothing can come out of nothing. Similarly, the modifications of unmoving objects are seen in moving objects in the shape of a variety of chyle etc. It is of course the use of these fruits etc. that brings about the wealth of the variety of forms etc. with animals. Similarly is seen the modifications of the animal into the plants.' (Vācaspati).

'This is subject to the limitations of time, space, form and disposing cause. Their natures do not manifest simultaneously' (*Vyāsa-bhāṣya*).

This is explained by Vācaspati as follows: Well, if all is of the nature of all, then everything being present everywhere, always and in all possible modes, even those results which do not exist simultaneously should manifest at once. For certainly when all the necessary causes of an effect are present it would not delay in its appearance. Hence it is said: This is subject to the limitation of space, time etc. Although everything can become the cause of everything yet the operation of the cause is limited by space. Thus Kāśmīra being the country of saffron, it will not grew in the Pāñcāla country, even though the other causes of its growth were all present there. Hence, saffron does not grow in the Pāñcāla and other countries. Similarly there are no rains in the summer season; therefore no growth of rice is possible in that season. Similarly a deer does not give birth to a man; because the form of a man cannot arise out of the form of a deer.

From this it is easy to see that there is a continual transformation from the inorganic earth, water etc. to the organic or the vegetable kingdom and from this again to the animal kingdom, and there is also a reverse process from the animal to the vegetable kingdom and from the vegetable to the inorganic elements.

Transformation, evolution or change means nothing but the displacement and re-arrangement of atoms in the constitution of the body, undergoing evolution or change. Time required for a unit of measure of time. In one such unit of time the whole universe being made up of atoms which are constantly vibrating and changing their places is undergoing change or transformation, evolution, birth, growth, decay.

Just as the smallest division of matter is called an atom, so the smallest division of time is called *kṣaṇa*, or rather a moment is the time taken by an atom to change its own unit of space and the continuity of such moments without break is what is meant by succession. The moments called past or future should all be regarded as being associated with change, so that in one moment of time the whole universe is undergoing change. The changes associated with each moment (consequent upon the displacement of the atoms) are regarded as the different attributes or qualities of the things.

Though we have seen that, according to *Vyāsa-bhāṣya*, things are not different from one another intrinsically and everything could be transformed into any other thing provided the necessary collocations could be arranged, yet it cannot be admitted that anything can really come out of any other thing and that there is actually a law to guide the course of evolution for we hear of a *pariṇāma-krama-niyama* or the law of a series of evolution. If we enquire into the nature of the origin of this law we find that space, time, causality and the atomic constitution of things (by virtue of which they can be classed into different substances) offer a resistance to the course of evolution which can never be overstepped. The energy which causes the displacement of atoms is not absolute in its power but has its power limited or arrested by space, time, causality and the definite constitution of things. The flow of energy causing evolution or change therefore has to accommodate itself and to follow the line of least resistence in the course of evolution determined by it. Thus there is no positive control over the evolving transformation consequent upon the flow of energy, but only the negative ones which curb and check the flow of energy from taking certain course. Thus it is said that a fruit at a certain point of space it occupies undergoes a development or a change that another fruit at another point of space, may not (commentary by Vācaspati on III.53).

About the transformation of energy from one state to another it is said that it takes place of itself, without the intervention from any other kind of agent, provided that there is no obstruction in the way. So the action of any other agent or efficient cause consists only in removing the obstacles or impediments in the way of the energy tending towards realising itself in its transformation. Thus it is said in the *Vyāsa-bhāṣya* (IV.3) the efficient cause does not move into effect the creative causes but only removes the obstacles or impediments, as by a farmer. As a farmer desirous of carrying water from an already well-filled bed to another does not draw the wəter with his own hand to places which are on the same or a lower level but simply removes the obstacles and thereupon the water flows down of itself to the other bed, so it removes the obstalces or impediments in the way of the development and thereby the creative causes naturally pass through the respective changes of themselves. Similarly, the same farmer does not possess the power of transferring the earth and the watery juices to the roots of rice in the same bed. What then? He weeds the *gavedhuka* and the *śyāmāka* out of the common bed and when they have been weeded out the juices themselves enter the roots of rice.

Thus we see that the energy conserved in one form naturally passes into another by manifesting consequent changes or transformations designated by the name of evolution. As this natural flow of energy is obstructed in various ways, by the resistance offered by space, time, form and causality, it has naturally to take the course in which there are no impediments and obstacles; at each stage new impediments may come in and interfere with the evolving process and compel the flow to change the direction of its course, so it is that we find that the evolutionary process has naturally to take curvilinear line rather than the straight one.

It is this resistance against the flow which compels it to reject thousands of courses open to it and select a particular one in which there is no resistance. It is this therefore that gives a *niyama* or regulation, restriction or limitation to the *pariṇāma-krama*, or the evolutionary succession.

The *pariṇāma-krama-niyama,* or the *deśakāla-krama-nimitto-pabandha* takes the question of the natural selection to a firmer basis and seeks to answer the question from the principle of conservation of energy. It seems to me that by attributing the resistance of nature to the particular atomic constitution of things and environments, it includes not only the modifications of the vegetable and the animal kingdom but also those of the inorganic world. It suggests that the force which guides the evolutionary process is not a peculiar thing different from other forces of nature, but reduces all forces to that of one kind generated by the continual displacement of the vibratory atoms of substance and the natural obstruction involved in the adoption of any mode of displacement, other than the one which belongs to the atoms owing to their particular constitutional arrangements and environments. Only that kind of evolution can result which has not to face the opposition of time, space or the particular atomic arrangements of things. For unless retarded by these the liberated energy will continue to form transformations which will again undergo a course of changes forced upon them by the varying retardations and oppositions either from the environments or from the peculiar nature of their own constitution.

To come to the question of the actual knowledge that the ancients had of the plant life and animal life, we find that the difference between the vegetable and the animal life has always been regarded as being one of degrees. Thus not only do we find in Manu that the plant life is spoken of as being creatures enveloped by a manifold darkness caused by past deeds and having an internal consciousness and also a capacity for enjoying pleasures and suffering pains, but we find that the *Mahābhārata* also speaks of the plants possessing all the ingredients with which men or the higher animals have been formed and also the five cognitive senses. As Bhṛgu replied to Bhāradvāja in the following words: As the trees flower and fructify, there must be *ākāśa* in the solid trees. As leaves, branches, flowers and fruits fade and die out through heat it must be admitted that the trees possess the sense of touch. As fruits and flowers suffer decay from the sounds of storms and thunder it must be admitted that the trees are possessed of the sense of hearing. Since a creeper encircles a tree and goes to all places it must be admitted that they are endowed with the power of vision, for without seeing they could not pursue a patch. Since the trees become cured of diseases and full of flowers by holy and unholy odours it must be admitted that they possess the sense of smell. Since they drink water from the roots and since they suffer from disease which again can be remedied it is to be admitted that they possess the sense of taste. As certain plants take water from upwards by mouth, like lotus stalks, so again, other trees drink water by their roots. Since the trees are subject to pleasure and pain and since they grow after coming out of the seed, I find life in plants and no unconsciousness. It is therefore that they take water and digest fire and air and by the digestion of food they become fatty and enjoy growth.

So far as the evolution of the trees from the inorganic world in concerned, I have not been able to come across any detailed account of it showing the stages through which the transformations actually take place from the inorganic to the organic, and also within the plant genus itself. It has been said of course in a general way that trees and creepers spring forth as modifications of the earth atom, but I have found nothing which shows the transitionary stages through which one class was transformed into another, so that we cannot know whether they had any definite views as to the manner in which the transformations actually take place. Relating to the question of structural botany, we find that in certain places the plants are said to be formed of the five elements, which are said to serve different purposes in constituting the plant body; thus the earth gives hardness to the plants, water gives smoothness, *tejas* heat to the plant body by which it assimilates its food; air causes plants to send forth its shoots; the *ākāśa* gives porosity and vacuity to plants; proper season also gives facility to the plants so that the various elements can develop the plant body at their best.

I have not however found the transition link where the inorganic has been supposed to pass into the organic, and I am not sure whether the ancients had any exact and definite notion about it. We find no doubt that the inorganic constitutes the body of the plant life, the five elements *kṣiti*, etc., constitute the body of the plant and serve diverse physiological purposes but we do not find the mention of any stage in which the inorganic imperceptibly passes into the organic. The question appears to have been studied by the ancients more in the light of conservation of energy than from any idea of showing the actual advance of the inorganic by slow marches towards the organic. Though some sort of an attempt at classification is seen of the plants in the form of *vanaspati*, *vṛkṣa*, *oṣadhi*, *tṛṇa*, *gulma*, etc., nothing whatever has been mentioned with regard to them from the point of view of evolution in its modern sense.

The mythical account of the *Purāṇas* however gives a somewhat different version of the order of evolution. Thus, according to the *Viṣṇupurāṇa*, first came the plants, next the animals, then the gods and then came the men. There instead of the word *pariṇāma* or evolution we find the word *sarga* or creation. It is however stated there that creation of God means only that God acted as the proximate cause whereas matter by the gradual realisation of its latent powers passed through various transformations which go by the name of evolution.

Plant evolution or creation is called there the *mukhya-sarga* or creation at its primary stage. The animal creation comes next and goes by the name of *tiryak-srota*. The creation of Gods is characterised as *arvāk-srota*. If we take the meaning of these words literally we see that after the *mukhya-sarga* or primary creation there is a deviation in the line of evolution in the production of animals, for *tiryak* means a curve. Then it seems that the cause of evolution took a higher or more improved turn and thus the gods were produced as a result thereof. Then from the gods by a lower turn *arvāk-srota* men were produced (see *Viṣṇupurāṇa* 1/4/50-52; 1/5/1-24; see also *Śrīmadbhāgavata*

III/10/13-26, where the same view is repeated in a slightly different form).

Animals have been classified in Suśruta as being of four kinds: generated from the plant world or the vegetables and thus called *udbhijja*; from moisture called *svedaja*; from the eggs called *aṇḍaja*; from the ovary called the *jarāyuja*. Dalhaṇa, the celebrated commentator of Suśruta, mentions certain other classes which he calls by the name of *yoni-saṅkara* or mixed species. Thus he says: since the classification of living beings has been differently read in different places, it is signified that there are cases of inter-admixture of species; thus among birds there is the species *valākā* which is found to come out from the eggs as well as from the ovaries. In the serpent species which generally come under the heading of *aṇḍaja* there is the subspecies, *ahipātaka* where are born from the ovary and do not belong to the class of *aṇḍaja* animals.

From this we see first of all that Suśruta knew that certain animals are generated from vegetable germs; secondly we see that at least Dalhaṇa knew that the species did not exist in a fixed order, but that there was also the mixture of the species. He does not of course argue that from these data it may be said that one species is gradually and imperceptibly merging into the other and that there is thus an evolution of one species from another, slowly going on through the intermediate transition links. But the fact that they did not think the species to be of a fixed order and that there were transition stages in which the lower and the higher species met, go to prove to some extent at least, that they were not totally unaware of the idea of evolution.

The principal feature of the doctrine of evolution with the orthodox schools consisted in this that though most of them would think the biological side of life to be a product of chemical synthesis or diverse self-grouping or re-arrangements of atoms, yet the whole dynamic of life was set in motion and in connection with and for the purposes of the soul. Thus we see that evolution in living being is just set up at the moment when it should become associated with the physical basis of evolution. Thus in Caraka we see that the development of the human embryo began just when the semen and the ovum came in contact in the womb of a female and at once the soul descended into it and the embryo was ready to develop.

It is said that the developing embryo is the joint product of (1) semen, (2) ovum, (3) wholesome and the hygenic habits of the parents (4) the nutritive juice of the digested food juice of the mother, and (5) soul. None of these can independently generate an embryo, but they all conjointly serve to generate it; just as a chariot is made out of the conjoint sustaining and productive action of its diverse parts, or a house is supported by the conjoint action of its four walls and the roof; so is developing embryo the result of the joint action of all the five causes just mentioned. It is also said that just as molten gold, copper, etc. assume the form of any mould in which they are poured, so the foetus assumes the shape of and develops in the form of a man or of any other animal according as the five causes of the foetus assemble in the body of an woman or of an animal.

The child produced out of the embryo is obliged to the mother's blood for its skin, blood, flesh, etc. To the semen of the father for hair, bone, etc. To its own eternal life principle or soul it owes the taking of birth as man or this or that animal, term of life, self-consciousness, mind, senses, inhalation, motor power, inhibiting power, figure, peculiarities of voice, colour, pleasure, pain, desire, antipathy, consciousness, retention, intelligence, memory, egoism and activity. In connection with it we may note that the mechanical, or physico-chemical transformation of semen-blood takes place in such a way as to suit the demands of the life principle. To the physiological habits of the parent it owes its general health, absence of idleness, want of greediness, the clearness of the function of the senses, the gift of voice, colour and strength and a happy temper. To the digested food juice of the mother, the child owes the formation of the body, growth, functional fullness, fullness of development, and energy.

If we remember how we began this discussion, we shall see that, in the evolution of matter, *tamas* and *rajas* played the most important parts whereas *sattva* remained latent. But such is the course of evolution that though in inorganic matter *sattva* had been completely overcome, yet it begins to find more and more scope in the ascending stages of the evolutionary process. Medhātithi explains this as follows: Though everything is made of the three *guṇas* yet with these *tamas* becomes supreme, and *sattva* and *rajas* become extremely subordinated; and so with the preponderance of *tamas* it ever suffers sorrow and disgust, the result of evil deeds. Since there is some *sattva* in them they enjoy some pleasure only. *Viṣṇupurāṇa* also characterises them as being Saṃvṛtātmā, enclosed souls.

Next to this state we find the animals which are described in *Viṣṇupurāṇa* as having a large proportion of *tamas* in them. Thus also the *Bhāgavata* characterises them as having no knowledge of past or future, full of darkness, being always engaged in satisfying animal wants such as eating etc., having the power of knowing things by smell and having within them no inquisitive spirit. Śrīdhara-svāmin further explains this state of existence by a quotation from *śruti*, saying that with animals hunger and thirst are their only knowledge. They can neither speak what they know nor can understand what they know. They do not know anything of the past nor what this world is and what this world is not. It is easy to see that they cannot have any sense of good or evil and are hence described as *bhogaśarīra*.

Even such a state is higher than the vegetable state of existence, just as the vegetable state was much higher than the ingorganic state. In this latter state the *sattva* was completely overcome whereas in the other two stages it showed signs of gradually recovering the lost ground.

In man however we find that *sattva* has its hindrances or limitations finally withdrawn. Hence we see that man lives in what may be called a universe of morality and intelligence. He has consciousness of all objects, internal or external, and has along with it the consciousness of his own. He not only perceives and conceives but thinks and argues. This peculiar aspect of evolution of greater and greater manifestation of *sattva* in the form of higher and higher development of intelligence and the moral qualities is attempted to be explained by the theory that this is due to the growing and growing resistance to *tamas*. Thus in Caraka we find that *sattva* has its full share in bringing about the development of the child by supplying a storehouse of moral and intellectual equipments for the child.

So it is that with the collocation of so many things that a foetus is generated. Thus we see that according to the variation of *sattva*, a man may vary to a very great extent. Some twenty different types of men have been spoken of and exemplified by Caraka.

It is also said that the constitution and temper of a man differs according to the peculiar kind of *sattva* that the man possesses. Thus we see that according to Caraka the moral endowments of a man have got an exact physical or physiological counterpart and that both of them correspond with each other.

Thus from just the moment that the foetus began to grow in the mother's womb the formation and the structure of its body adopted particular modes or moments of development according to the particular moral and intellectual endowments which it will be the role of the man's body to manifest. It is therefore the moral and the intellectual endowments that the man is destined to possess hereafter and have the power to influence and regulate the development of his body from the earliest stage of the growth of the foetus. It will be easy to see that the assertions of Caraka have laid the basis of physiological psychology, though we are sorry to notice that further particular on the subject cannot be found in his work.

We discussed that the developing foetus is the joint product of several causes which have already been enumerated. The child owes the different parts of its body to the different causes in a joint state of activity and these also we have enumerated above.

Now the defect of any one of these causes of any kind may be expected to produce a defect in the corresponding part of the body which the child owes to that cause. But Caraka says that defect of any kind does not necessarily affect the child, but only those defects which affect any part of the seed or embryo which was destined to grow and develop into a particular limb and show their influence and affect the growth of that particular limb of the child. Any and every defect does not necessarily affect the seed part; so only such defects as affect the seed part of any particular limb really injure that particular part of the child's body or limb which owed its existence to the growth or development of that part of the embryo which had been injured by the defect of any of the joint causes.

We have seen that the different parts of the embryo are the products of the different causes acting together in unison. There is the father's part of the semen, from which are produced those parts of embryo which develop into bones, hair, etc. There is the mother's part or the ovum from which are produced those parts of the embryo which would later on develop into skin, flesh, etc. There is also the soul to which the general activity of the embryo, the senses, pleasure, pain, etc. are due and these would necessarily vary according to the different kinds of previous *karmas* or actions with which the soul is associated in that particular birth. Then there are the hygienic habits of the parent which manifest in the health activity of the child, and these hygenic habits being affected in any way, the health and activity of the child are affected too in that particular way. Again a defect of the *sattva* part of the embryo of any kind shows iteself through the embryo by producing a corresponding moral and intellectual incapacity of the child. Thus it is easy to see that the inheritance of the child comes from all the six causes acting in unison and not from any one of them merely; the inheritance is again limited to the extent to which the causes themselves can transmit them to the seed part or the embryo. The peculiarities of the parent, whether acquired or non-acquired, can all be transmitted to the child provided it has affected or influenced the seed part; that being represented that it might be transmitted to the child. Only that part of the causes can be transmitted or inherited which passes to the seed part of the embryo. So it does not necessarily follow that the son of a fool will necessarily be a fool, for intelligence etc. cannot be inherited from the father generally but belongs to the soul or the *sattva* part of the embryo. Thus Caraka says : It has been argued that if man is produced from man, how is it that those who are born of foolish father do not necessarily become foolish like their father? When any part of the seed which represents any particular part or limb of the child is affected, then that part or limb of the child is affected too; if the seed is unaffected then that part or limb also remains unaffected.

So both the alternatives are possible. A child may or may not be affected by his father's defect. With all children, the senses they owe to themselves, and the reason of the defect or goodness depends upon accident or moral destiny. It is therefore that children born of fools may or may not be fools like their father, Caraka illustrates this theory again: The inheritance is qualitatively limited by the degree in which it can transmit itself to the seed part. Thus it is said that if in the blood of the mother there be a defect of such a nature that it can affect that part of the embryo only which can develop into the ovary of the child, then only the ovary of the child would be affected and the child would be barren.

The child owes his body to the parents whereas for all his mental and moral endowments he is not in any way obligated to his parents. He has got them for himself. Only the body of the child is inherited from the body of the parents (through semen and blood) and the food juice of the mother. Only such of the habits of the parents which can modify or affect their semen and blood in such a way as to give it any particularity of any kind will be able to show them in fashioning the growth of the embryo in a particular form, and thereby cause the child to inherit them the peculiar formation of his constitution. It is therefore that the *sātmya* or the hygienic habits of the parent can be inherited by the child in the healthy or unhealthy constitution of the body, whereas any other kind of moral or intellectual habits of the parents are not generally inherited by the child. About inheriting his body also, the child is responsible for some parts of his body to his father and for other parts to his mother. So the defect or goodness of those parts of the body of the father or mother which will not be transmitted to the foetus can never be inherited by him from his father or mother. Thus, for example, the child owes its stomach to his mother and not to his father. So any defect or goodness of the father's stomach is not likely to be inherited by the child; for it is not represented in the semen of the father which goes to form a part of the embryo.[38]

The Unity of the Evolution of Man with That of the Universe

Caraka says that the evolution and nature of man resembles the evolution and nature of the Universe. All kinds of concrete existence in the Universe find their exact parallels or counterparts in the human system. Caraka further says that the course of production, growth, decay and destruction of the Universe and that of man are exactly the same. Thus the Universe is made up of the same *dhātus* and so is the man; the process of evolution, generation or production of the Universe and of man are all the same. This evolution of course includes both production and growth and we have seen above that the same law of *pariṇāma* which guides the Universe, guides also the evolution of man. The laws of decay and destruction are also the same. For as all evolution is due to the liberation of *rajas* or energy and reintegration of the atoms of the five elements followed by more and more differentiated and determinate character of the whole. So all destruction is the product of the liberation of energy and disintegration of parts followed by more and more undifferentiated indeterminate character of the parts and of the whole.

Reintegration of parts is the soul of evolution, while separation, *vibhāga* of parts, disintegration of parts is the principal thing in destruction. Thus to summarise: We see that the course of evolution begins with the three reals—*sattva* (intelligence stuff), *rajas* (energy) and *tamas* (obstructing factor). They by their combination generate the Tanmātras. From the *tanmātras* the atoms are generated. With the atoms we come to the *bhūtas*. The *pariṇāma* or evolution consists in this stage in the displacement and the mutual rearrangement of the atoms. All the multifarious kinds of the inorganic world of objects are the products of the displacements and rearrangements acting according to a definite law. At a certain stage of the development of the inorganic world an altogether new factor called soul intervenses and this factor, soul, though absolutely inactive in itself is the goal for which all the activities of life are perserved and produced, which are in themselves but material products. With the introduction of life by the influence of soul and its vital powers different bodies evolve, suitable to such animal, until we come to man, where we find the soul wedded to the most perfect body of evolution. Man's body so far as it is a physical object is like any other object of nature passing through the process of evolution. But the introduction of soul from the organic stage marks the epoch of a new kind of progress. This epoch attains it as highest achievement when it comes to the moral being. So far as the physical world is concerned there is the same law of evolution from the relatively less differentiated, less determinate, less coherent whole to the relatively more differentiated, more determinate, more coherent whole and looked at from this point of view man's life and body are but a part of the universe suffering the same process of growth and decay. But looked at from another point of view all living beings and man, preeminently by virtue of his soul, is a person and this addition of personality is a decisive addition. Thus so far as the physical parts and the biological sides of life are concerned he is an object of nature, but so far as his soul is concerned he is a person and it is this personality which constitutes his spirituality, the growth and evolution of which may be traced in art, religion, society and state. According to the Sāṅkhya-Pātañjala schools, salvation comes in when man knows that every other thing, every other process, belongs to the natural and material order, and suffer their changes. Soul alone is the actionless, passionless entity for the enjoyment and liberation of which the whole material order moves in diverse lines. It is this freedom of the soul and its realisation that constitutes the salvation of man, the goal of the world destiny.

APPENDIX

Genesis of the Tanmatras

The genesis of the *bhūtas* from the *tanmātras* and the Tanmātras from the *ahaṅkāra* or ego and the *ahaṅkāra* from the Buddhi-tattva has sometimes misled scholars to suppose that, according to the Sāṅkhya philosophy, matter has been derived from thoughts and ideas. Thus as it is observed: 'There has been much confusion in the West as to the exact nature of this standard. It derives the material from the mental or the physical, that is to say, from things which are of the nature of thoughts and ideas and feelings. But in spite of this fact Prof. Garbe who is perhaps the only scholar in the West who has made a thorough study of the literature of this standard, has yet taken it to be a form of materialism; so much so that he has seen no place for psychology in its stead. This is indeed strange not only because it is absolutely against the universal tradition of the Hindus, but also because it is absurd to call a system of philosophy materialistic which derives matter from thoughts and ideas.'

From the description of the genesis as is generally found in the Sāṅkhya compendiums such an idealistic explanation of the Sāṅkhya doctrines is not however altogether improbable. But if we look at it in connection with the most important passage on the subject in the *Vyāsa-bhāṣya*, the whole system seems to assume such a position that it can neither be called altogether materialistic nor idealistic in the ordinary senses of the term. For here we see that the separation, evolution or determination of *mahat* takes place in such a way that it remains itself integrated with the *prakṛti* all the while. Mahat is therefore not posited in opposition to the *prakṛti* as its differentiated evolute. What we find here is rather the differentiation from the *prakṛti* but which is at the same time integrated with it. The course of evolution here described points out that in each stage it is the *prakṛti* hereself which becomes more differentiated and the determinate and coherent. The evolution of *mahat* means that the absolute equilibrium of the *prakṛti* being negated and broken, there is the predominance of the Sattva which justifies its christening with the new names *mahat*, *sattva*, *liṅga*, or *sattvamātra*. This differentiation cannot however be thought of from the aspect of its integration with the *prakṛti*. Increasing differentiation goes on along with increasing integration within the evolving whole and by this double process, from what was an incoherent, indeterminate, homogeneous whole, evolves the *mahat*. *Mahat* can never be regarded as the product of *prakṛti* outside of it but is the *prakṛti* which has been differentiated within itself in order to be more and more integrated with itself; there is *viveka* or determination in *saṃsṛṣṭi* or integration. We find that the *ahaṅkāra* and the five *tanmātras* are differentiated in like manner. It is said no doubt that the five *tanmātras* are evolved from the ego or the *ahaṅkāra*, but this evolution cannot be regarded to be of the same kind at the evolution of the *bhūtas* from the Tanmātras or of the senses from the ego. With the evolution of the stadium of *mahat* there is an oscillation consequent upon the liberation of *rajas* which takes three different courses according to the predominance of *sattva*, *rajas* or *tamas*. The transformation which *mahat* undergoes by this liberation of *rajas* is called the ego or *ahaṅkāra*. The liberated *rajas* gives at one moment a shake to *sattva* and asserts its own predominance and thus the differentiation which is the product of the liberation of the *rajas* though associated with it represents the root of the development of this stadium in three distinct directions. Thus according to these three phases the ego is called *sāttvika*, *rājasika*, and *tāmasika*. There different phases represent the disturbance caused in the three constituent entities or *guṇas* of *mahat* which will lead the ego to develop in three distinct directions. The ego however in spite of its differentiation with itself has become more determinate and coherent in the form of the Ego and has thus become integrated with itself in a new form. But it is said that the five *tanmātras* together with the ego are evolved from the *mahat*.

To understand all this clearly we must remember that the *tanmātras* are generated with successive accretions from the *bhūtādi*; thus from the *bhūtādi* the rudiment matter by the action of *rajas*, the *śabdatanmātra* or the sound potential being generated there is an accretion of *bhūtādi* and by the action of *rajas* the touch-potential is produced and so on; each new *tanmātra* is generated at each successive accretion. We must also remember that though *bhūtādi* or the *tamas* side of *ahaṅkāra* is regarded as being one with the conception of the ego or *ahaṅkāra*, there being a preponderance of *tamas*, is essentially different in nature from the *sattva* side of *ahaṅkāra*. Its inclusion in *ahaṅkāra* with the other two phases is due to the fact that all the three phases of them are associated and taken up, in the very first moment of the oscillatory movement in the *mahat*. The successive accretion of *tamas* for the formation of the *tanmātras* are made from the *mahat* through the *bhūtādi*; or rather the *bhūtādi* represents the *tamas* side of *mahat* which is in a state of activity by the inherent *rajas* side of activity for the formation of the *tanmātras*. *Bhūtādi* is the *tamas*, rudiment matter, mass, just when we conceive it to be unmoved by *rajas* for the formation of the *tanmātras* by successive collocations of gradual accretions and their definite combinations. It is the transitional state through which differentiations and determination of *tamas* take place with the help of *rajas* in the very body of the *mahat* with which they are integrated. These determinations cannot be conceived in any way as being outside of *mahat*. In the production of the atoms however from the *tanmātras* the differentiation and integration take place in the *tanmātras* and not in *mahat*; so also the differentiation and integration which result in the production of the senses, the conative and the cognitive and *manas*, take place directly in the body of the ego and not in the *mahat*. Those *tattvas* or categories the genesis of which depends directly upon the differentiation and integration of the *mahat* are classed as *aviśeṣas*. Though the *tanmātras* are derived from *ahaṅkāra* yet the very fact that the basis of their originating collocations lie directly in the *mahat* makes in idealistic explanation of the Pātañjala doctrine an impossibility. This point however has been lost sight of by the later Sāṅkhya interpretors, but that this had been the earlier Sāṅkhya doctrine is suggested by the inconsistency pointed out by Śaṅkara in his refutation of the doctrine (*Vedānta-bhāṣya*, II.2.10). Intentionally or unintentionally Śaṅkara did not try to reconcile there the seeming contradictions of the production of the *tanmātras* from *mahat* and also from Ahaṅkāra but only threw them in the face of the Sāṅkhyists. Vācaspati, Govindānanda and Ānandagiri however are all silent upon this point. It seems however that Vācaspati himself is inclined to explain Sāṅkhya from another point of view and seeks to explain their genesis on Fichte's lines or rather from the point of view of Vedāntic idealism.

The three stages of *bhūtādi*, *tanmātras* and the atoms have thus been described by Dr. B.N. Seal. 'The ultimate constitution of matter is a question of the profoundest interest in the Sāṅkhya-Pātañjala system. Three stages clearly stand out in the genesis of matter:– (1) the original infinitesimal units of mass or inertia, absolutely homogeneous and ubiquitous, on which energy does work, when the original equilibrium comes to an end (*bhūtādi-tāmasa-ahaṅkāra*); (2) the infra-atomic unit potentials charged with different kinds of energy, which result from the action of energy on the original units of mass (*tanmātras*) and (3) the five different classes of atoms, the minutest divisions of which gross matter is capable, but which are themselves complex *tanmātric* systems (*sthūlabhūtaparamāṇu*).

'The first stadium, *bhūtādi*, is absolutely homogeneous and absolutely inert, being devoid of all physical and chemical characters (*rūpādibhirasaṃyutam*) except quantum or mass (*paricchinnatva*, *parimāṇa*); and this admits neither of addition nor of substraction, can neither be created nor destroyed. The second stadium, *tanmātra*, represents subtile matter, vibratory impingent radiant, etc. instinct with 'potential' energy. These potentials arise from the unequal aggregation of the original mass units in different proportions and collocations with an unequal distribution of the original energy (*rajas*). The *tanmātras* possess something more than quantum of mass and energy; they possess physical characters; some of them penetrability (*avakāśadāna*), other powers of impact or pressure, other radiant heat, others again capability of viscous and cohesive attraction. In intimate relation of these physical characters they also possess the potentials of the energies represented by sound, touch, colour, taste and smell; but being subtile matter, they are devoid of the peculiar forms which these 'potentials' assume in particles of gross matter like the atoms and their aggregates. In other words, the potentials lodged in subtile matter must undergo peculiar transformations by new groupings or collocations to be classed among sensory stimuli—gross matter being supposed to be matter endowed with the properties of the class of sensory stimuli though in the minutest particles thereof the sensory stimuli may be infra-sensible.

'The *tanmātras* then are infra-atomic particles charged with specific potential energies. First, the potential of the sound stimulus is lodged in one class of particles, *tanmātras* which possess the physical energy of vibration (*parispanda*) and serve to form the radicle of the ether atom (*ākāśaparamāṇu*); then the potential of the tactile stimulus is lodged in another class of *tanmātras*, particles which possess the physical energy of impact or mechanical pressure, in addition to that of vibration and serve to form the radicle of the air-atom (*vāyuparamāṇu*); next, the potential of the colour stimulus is lodged in a third class of *tanmātras*, particles which are charged with the energy of radiant heat and light, in addition to those of impact and vibration, and serve to form the nucleus of the light and heat corpuscles; then the potential of the taste stimulus is lodged in other *tanmātras*, particles which possess the energy of viscous attraction, in addition to those of heat, impact and vibration, and which afterwards develop into the atom of water; and, lastly, the potential of the smell stimulus is lodged in a further class of *tanmātras*, particles which are charged with the energy of cohesive attraction, in addition to those of viscous attraction, heat, impact, and vibration and which serve to form the radicle of the earth-atom.'[39]

A very wide divergence of views is however found about the genesis of the *tanmātras*; thus, according to *Viṣṇupurāṇa*, *bhūtādi* in conjunction produces the sound potential and this in conjunction with *bhūtādi* produces the *ākāśa-paramāṇu.* This Ākāśa-paramāṇu in conjunction with *bhūta* produces the touch potential and that in conjunction with *bhūta* produces the *vāyu* atom. Parāśara again says that the *śabda-tanmātra* is produced from the *bhutadi* and from the *śabda-tanmātra* is produced the *sparśa-tanmātra*, and from it the *rūpa-tanmātra* and so on. From *śabdatanmātra* as centre surrounded by *bhūtādi*, the *ākāś-paramāṇu* is generated; from *śabdatanmātra* as centre surrounded by *sparśa-tanmātra* and the *ākāśa* and the *vāyu paramāṇu* is produced, from *rūpatanmātra* similarly with *sparśatanmātra* and the *vāyu paramāṇu tejas* is generated and so on.

About the characteristics of the *tanmātras* it is however important to note that though they are sufficiently differentiated to be classed as *kṣiti*, *ap*, *tejas*, *marut* or *vāyu*, they are not yet in themselves sensible but rudiments by the peculiar combination of which the atoms or the sensible elements are produced.

Notes

1. siddhaṃ tu yasya guṇasya bhāvād dravye śabdaniveśas tadabhidhāne tvatalau. siddham etat. katham? yasya guṇasya bhāvād dravye śabdaniveśas tadabhidhāne tasmin guṇe vaktavye pratyayena bhavitavyam. kiṃ punar dravyam, kiṃ punar guṇāḥ? śabdasparśarūparasagandhā guṇās tato'nyad dravyam. kiṃ punar anyacchabdādibhyo dravyam āhosvid ananyat? guṇasyāyaṃ bhāvād dravye śabdaniveśaṃ kurvan khyāpayati anyat śabdādibhyo dravyam iti. ananyat śabdādibhyo dravyam. na hyanyad upalabhyate. anyacchabdādibhyo dravyam. tat tvanumānagamyam. tad yathā oṣadhivanaspatīnāṃ vṛddhihrāsau, jyotiṣāṃ gatir iti. ko'sāvanumānaḥ? iha samāne varṣmaṇi pariṇāhe ca anyat tulāgraṃ bhavati lohasya anyat kārpāsānāṃ yatkṛto viśeṣas tad dravyam. tathā kaścit spṛśanneva chinatti kaścit lambamāno'pi na chinatti. yatkṛto viśeṣas tad dravyam. tathā kaścid ekenaiva prahāreṇa vyapavargaṃ karoti kaścid dvābhyām api na karoti. yatkṛto viśeṣas tad dravyam. atha vā yasya guṇāntareṣu api prādurbhavatsu tattvaṃ na vihanyate tad dravyam. kiṃ punaḥ tattvam? tadbhāvas tatvam. tad yathā āmalakādīnāṃ phalānāṃ raktādayaḥ pītādayaś ca guṇāḥ prādurabhavanti, āmalakaṃ vadaram ityeva bhavati. anvarthaṃ khalvapi nirvacanaṃ guṇasaṃdrāvo dravyam iti. *Mahābhāṣya* on v.i. 199.
2. See Patañjali's *Mahābhāṣya* on i.2.64 and v.1.59.
3. ātmā vastu svabhāvaśca śarīraṃ tattvam ityapi dravyam ityasya paryāyās tacca nityamiti smṛtam//—*Vākyapadīya*, III.2.1.
4. Helārāja on *ibid.* III. 2. 11.
5. *Vākyapadīya* III. 2. 12
6. Editor's note : In the manuscript of S.N. Dasgupta, we find here a reference to *Abhidharmakośa*, III p. 100 a-b. However, in the printed edition of the text as edited by Dvarikadas Sastri (Benares 1971), we have failed to trace exactly this view in the third *Kośasthāna* defended by Vasubandhu, specially about the arrangement of the atoms, though it is suggested that an *aṇu* is equal in measure to seven *paramāṇus*. On the contrary, as it is well known, in verse 12 of Vasubandhu's *Vijñaptimātratāsiddhi*, it is argued against the atomic hypothesis that the partless atoms, if admitted, a combination of the six atoms will have to be further accepted and hence also the six parts of the atom to explain the atomic combination.
7. The reals of the intelligence-stuff have been omitted in this connection as they are relatively unimportant in conceiving the constitution of matter.
8. See *Viśeṣāvaśyaka-bhāṣya*, pp. 1052-1062.
9. The Buddhists hold that there are four primary colours, viz. blue, yellow, red and white. See quotation from *Abhidharma Kośa Śāstra* in Yamakmi Sogen's *Systems of Buddhistic Thought*, p. 143.
10. See *Viśeṣāvaśyaka-bhāṣya*.
11. *Ibid.*

12. *Ibid.*
13. Editor's note: Admitting this well-known Nyāya-Vaiśeṣika argument, it is claimed that divisibility culminates in the perceptible *trasareṇu* and not in imperceptible *paramāṇu* of the Vaiśeṣikas.
14. Our experience of the heavenly bodies as remaining unchanged is an illusion, but since the composition of the light cannot be proved to be due to the breaking up of the flame into particles, there was no reason for supposing that our experience of the sun etc., as remaining unchanged was an illusion. Moreover, in a ray of light none of the substances such as the wick or the oil is seen that we could regard it as the broken parts of flames. if it is said that just as the flowers emit fragrant particles and yet remain unchanged so we may consider light as being due to the emission of corpuscles from flaming objects; but Veṅkaṭa objects to it and says that the answer just given applies to the present example as well; moreover, in the case of fragrance it may be imagined that the odour particles are carried by the wind and they last even when the flowers are destroyed, but not so the light substance; of course in summer nights heat is felt though the source of light is absent; a pencil of light is just as it is seen—thick at the root and thin at the end. Barada and Viṣṇumiśra have indeed spoken of light rays as being without parts but that means that it has no such parts (as other things have) which may be split or touched or broken. It does not exist independently of flaming objects which produce it. According to the difference in the nature of the source from which it proceeds it can perform diverse functions such as drying, expanding, heating (chemical or otherwises), illuminating, etc., in different degrees of intensity.
15. See Govardhana's *Nyāyabodhinī* (pp. 9, 10) on *Tarkasaṃgraha*. Nirnaya Sagar Press, Bombay, 1917.
16. See Uddyotakara's *Vārttika* and Vātsyāyana's *Bhāṣya* on NS. III. 1.4.
17. The ray from the eye strikes against mirrors, water, etc; the ray on returning is associated with one's face; the image is seen in the prolongation of the direction in which the reflected ray returns. Uddyotakara's *Vārttika*, on NS. III. 1.49.

    See also *Siddhāntaleśa*, pp. 60-62 (Vizianagram edition).
18. Things which are not in contact with the senses cannot be touched, but yet there may be (in the case of light) either direct penetration or a bent course (just as water oozes out through the pores of an earthen vessel either directly or through a refracted course). Vātsyāyana and Uddyotakara on NS. III. 1.47.

    In the *Siddhānataleśa* also reference is found to bent course of light: p. 61. It cannot be held that the face upon shoulder cannot be directly perceived for when the rays are reflected from the surface or mirror it turns back and grasps the object of reflection in a bent course like a creeper.
19. There are four kinds of *tejas*. First, that which has both colour and touch like the ray of the sun. Secondly, that which has no touch but only colour like the ray of a lamp. Both these have colour as their rays possess the manifest colour properties. Thirdly, that which has tangible heat

property only, but no visible colour, as in the case of heat in water. Fourthly, that which has neither the tangible property of heat nor visibility as colour, as the ray of light that starts from the eye. None of these two latter is visible because they have neither colour nor visibility.

20. In the atoms of water and *tejas* colour exists eternally. Again, the natural eternal colour of the *tejas* substance was regarded as being white; its visible red or brown colour is due to its association with other matters. Its touch is also always hot (though, of course, it could sometimes exist in an unmanifested form). *Nyāyakandalī* on Praśastapāda's *Bhāṣya,* Dravyagrantha, p. 39, (Vizianagram series edn.).
Sun's *tejas* which is the cause of all *pāka* changes cannot be removed by cold. See *Kiraṇāvali* of Udayana, Sṛṣṭi-saṃhāra-vidhinirūpaṇa. In the heat of the sun, the same process is seen.
21. See *Nyāya-siddhāñjana*, p. 31.
22. See *Nyāyakandalī*, pp. 40-41.
23. See *Tātparya-ṭīkā.* (Benares edn.), p. 78
24. Heaviness is the nature of things that cause them to fall of themselves.
25. *Mahābhāṣya* on i. 1.49.
26. See *Vākyapadīya* iii. 7.
27. *Ibid.*, iii. 1.
28. p. 12.
29. It is through mere imagination that even in the case of motionless things the forms of succession of events as independent and dependent are manifested.

    All things are without any motion, energy is different from them; the cases are those which are called the agents and instruments which make actions appear as dependent on others; the actions manifest themselves in successive moments; but all these appearances are due to the wrong habit of the intellect through a beginningless series of false ways of thinking. See *Vākyapadīya*, pp. 173-180.
30. See *Nyāyakandalī*, Karma-grantha.
31. See *Nyāya-siddhāñjana*, pp. 176-177.
32. See *Tattva-muktākalāpa* and *Sarvārtha-siddhi.*
33. The above sketch has mainly been based on J.H. Poynting's brilliant contribution to Hastings' *Encyclopaedia of Religion and Ethics* on *Atomic Theory: Medieval and Modern*, vol. 2, pp. 203-210. Editor's note. In fact, the entire section is a summary of this article usually retaining its original language.
34. *Svetāśvatara*, *Maitrī*, etc.
35. *Chāndogya Upaniṣad*, VI.
36. Editor's note: The quotation is from B.N. Seal, *The Positive Sciences of the Ancient Hindus*, London, 1915, pp. 7-8.
37. *Editor's note*: *ibid.*, p. 46.
38. *Editor's note*: In the manuscript left by Professor Dasgupta, apparently without thoroughly revising it, we find this discussion of the question of foetal development as understood by the Āyurvedic school much prolonged and with considerable repetitions. Since however in the second volume

of his *History of Indian Philosophy* the discussion of the same subject is to be found in a very systematic form along with appropriate textual references, we have preferred to skip over in the present book this part of the manuscript and to move on to the main theme of the present part of his manuscript, namely, the theories of cosmic changes.

39. Editor's note: B.N. Seal, *op. cit.*, pp. 24-26.

Index

Abhidharma Kośa Śāstra 6-7
Ākāśa, 11; characteristics, 66,68
Akṣara, 11
Ānandagiri, 87
Ap; characteristics, 66, 68
Apyayadikṣita, 13
Aristotle, 2; doctrine of 'natural places' of thing, 16
Arthaśāstra, 58
Atom (paramāṇu), 7, 25, 87, 88, 90; character, 63; classification, 8-9; combination, 10; earth, 62; latest conception, 35-36; physical movement, 69-70; smallest division of matter, 71; spherical shape, 62; water, 62; valency, 10; *vāyu* or *tejas*, 62
Atomic doctrines; concept of Nyāya-Vaiśeṣika, 14
Atomic motion, 25
Atomic theory, 10-11, 19; in Greece, 38
Avogardo; hypothesis, 33, 36
Avyakta, 11

Bacon; concept of elements, 30
(The) Bauddha; heterodox system, 55
Bernovilli (1738); concept of corpuscles, 31
Bhāgavata, 78
Bharadvāja, 74
Bhartṛhari, 5, 22; concept of matter, 16
Bhāskara; concept of gravity, 26; matter, 18; time, 45
Bhṛgu, 74
Bhūta, 61-62, 68, 69, 85, 86, 87, 88, 89; molecules contain two atoms, 59; qualities, 66; structure, 67
Black, 33
Boltzmann, 33
Boscovich; hypothesis, 31-32
Boyle, Robert (1627-1691); concept of matter, 30-31
Brahmadeva, 45
(*The*) *Bṛhadāraṇyaka*, 53
(*The*) *Bṛhat-saṃhitā*, 59
(The) Buddhist; concept of *ākāśa*, 59; atom, 11; elements, 43; matter, 6-7; space, 44

Caraka, 64, 78, 79; concept of ākāśa, 66; evolution of nature and man, 81-82; five *bhūtas*, 66-67; human embryo, 76-77, 78, 79, 80, 81
Cārvāka; concept of life, 55-56
Cavendish, 33
(*The*) *Chāndogya Upaniṣad*, 53, 55
Corpuscular theory, 60
Crookes, 35
Change; views of Vaiśeṣikas and Naiyāyikas, 62
Chemical changes, 14
Chemical philosophy, 33
Claussius, 33
Coherent (*yutasiddha*), 65
Compound forms (*skandha*), 8
Conglomerations of energy (*śakti-samāhāra-mātram ghāṭadayah*), 22
Continuity (*varttana*), 45

Dalhaṇa, 68, 76
Dalton, 33, 36
Democritus, 36, 38; concept of atom, 43; matter, 29-30
Deśakāla-krama-nimittopabandha, 73
Descartes; indivisibility of atom, 30, 31
Determinate (*viśeṣa*), 65
Differentiated (*vaiṣamya*), 65

Ego (*ahaṅkāra*), 85, 86, 87
Empedocles (c. 450 B.C.); principles of the four elements, 29

Empiricists or Realists, 46-47
Energy (*rajas*), 69-70; conservation, 63; distribution, 67-68; transformation, 72-73
Epicurus, 38; concept of atom, 30
Evolution; man, 81-82; matter, 77-78
(The) Evolutionists; (The) Sāṅkhya-Yoga and the Vaiṣṇavas, 46

Faraday, 35; concept of atom, 32
Forms; anudbhūta and udbhūta, 14

Gaṇitasārasaṁgraha, 45
Garbe (Prof.), 85
Gautama, 59
Govardhana, 12, 13
Govindānanda, 87
(The) grammar school, 46; concept of space, 44
Gravity, 26; obstruction (*pratibandhakatā*), 26
(The) Greek; atomic theory, 36-37; life, 2; philosophers' conception of matter, 29-30
(The) *Guṇa*; doctrine, 41

Heat; effect on molecule, 13
Heaviness (*guru*), 7
Hegel, 58
Helārāja, 16, 22; explains the view of Patañjali, 5
(The) Hellenic; spirit, 2; times, 2
Helmholtz, 34
Heraclitus; concept of change, 29
Higgins, William, 33
Hindu; chemistry, 3; medicine, 3; physics, 3; philosophical speculations, 3

(The) Idealistic system, 57
(The) Idealists; followers of Gauḍapāda or Śaṅkara, Mādhyamikas, Yogācāras, 46
Incoherent (*ayutasiddha*), 65
Indian; philosophy and its expression, 2; religion, 2
Indeterminate (*aviśeṣa*), 65
Iśvarakṛṣṇa, *kārikā*, 58

Jaina; classification of atoms, 9-10; combination of atoms, 10; concept of elements, 43; matter, 43; matter and their properties, 7-9; philosophy, 18; systems, 55
Jayanta, 13
Joule; kinetic theory, 33

Kanāda, 57, 59; on the system of Vaiśeṣika, 57
Kant, 58
Kapila, 57, 64
Kauṭilya, 58
Kelvin (Lord), 32, 34
Kinetic theory, 34
Kronig, 33
Kṣaṇa; smallest division of time, 71
Kumārila, 59; concept of energy, 24; *śakti*, 24

Lormor, 34
Leucippus, 36; atomic theory, 38; matter and atoms, 29-30
Life; conglomeration of atoms, 57; nihilists view, 55-56
Light; property, 11-12
Light-heat substance; concept of Nyāya-Vaiśeṣika and the Vaiṣṇava school, 14
Lokāyata (popular view), 56

Mādhavāchārya; unit of time, 45
Mahābhārata, 58; speaks of the plants, 74
Mahābhāṣya, 4, 5, 15, 21, 46
Manu; concept of the plant life, 73
Mass (*dravya*), 5; *Tanmātras*, 88
Mass (*tamas*) and energy (*rajas*), 41-42
Matter (*dravya*), 6; composition, 65; existence, 8; explanation of Sāṃkhya-Pātañjala system, 88-89; the grammar school, 19; the Nyāya-Vaiśeṣika, 19; the Śaivas, 19;

Sāṃkhya-Yoga, 19; Tāntrikas, 19; Vaiṣṇava as represented by Veṅkaṭa, 19; divisibility, 11
Matter and energy; relation, 6
Matter and motion, 37-38; concept of the Hindus, 3; modern ideas, 37-38; salient points, 48; theory of the Hindus, 38-43; Indian sages, 37
Matter and spirit, 32
Matter or mass; 3-4
Māyā, 10
Maxwell, 33
Medhātithi; stages of the evolutionary process, 78
(The) Mimāṃsā school, 24; concept of motion, 27; elements, 43-44
Miśra, Vācaspati, 66
Molecule; combinations, 10; forms of, 12, 33-34; formation, 59; view, 62; quality, 63
Motion (*karma*), 24-25; classification in the Nyāya-Kandali, 27; concept of Nāgārjuna (2nd century A.D.), 19-21; Patañjali, 21-23; difference between Vaiśeṣika and Veṅkaṭa, 28-29; momentum (*Saṃskāras*), 25-26

Nāgārjuna; concept of motion, 19-21
(The) Naiyāyikas; view of atom, 47
Nature (*svabhāva*), 5
Newton; concept of atom, 32; *principia*, 31
Nyāyabodhinī; concept of heat, colour and taste, 60; commentary on Annam Bhaṭṭa's *Tarkasaṃgraha*, 60
Nyāyakandali, 6; perception of time, 44; rotatory motion, 27
Nyāya; change of matter, 13; concept of motion, 26, 27; light and heat, 12; theory of compounds, 47
Nyāya-Vaiśeṣika, 61, 63; concept of atom, 9; element, 47, motion, 28, space, 44; kinds of matter-atoms, 18; phenomenon of light, 19; principle of metaphysics, 17; quality of atoms, 15; *tejas*, 14; theories, 59; time, 46

Orthodox schools, 59
Padārthatattva-nirūpana, 6

Pāka (heat), 12; influence of atoms, 12
Pāñcāla, 71
Pāṇini, 17
Pariṇāma-krama-niyama, 65, 70, 71-72, 73
Patañjali, 4, 5, 15-16, 28, 57, 64, 87; concept of gravity, 17, 26; mass and matter, 14, motion, 21-23; time, 46; school, 58
Phlogistic and anti-phlogistic theories, 33
(The) Philosophical system; difference between India and Europe, 57-83
Plato, 2
Plum (*Āmlaka*), 4
Poynting, 32
Power (*śakti*), 5, 16, 22
Prakṛiti, 10, 11
Praśastapāda, 13
Priestly, 33; concept of atom, 32
Pṛthivī; characteristics, 66
(*The*) *Purāṇas*, 51
(*The*) *Puruṣasūkta*, 53
(The) Pythagoreans, 29

Qualities (*guṇas*); difference with thing (*dravya*), 3-4

Raghunātha Śiromaṇi; concept of matter, 6
Rahasya Śāstra, 16
Rankine, 34
Ray, P.C. (Dr.), 3
Reality (*tattva*), 5
Religion, Society and State, 83
(The) Ṛgveda, 38
Rūpa, 68

Śabda, 68

Śakti; concept of Kumārila, 24
Śaṅkarāchārya, 58, 59, 87
Śaṅkaramiśra, 13
(The) Sāṅkhya schools, 11, 57, 58, 63, 64, 65, 88; concept of *ākāśa*, 59; doctrine, 87; mass and energy, 42, 43; material world, 64; matter, 7; motion, 27-28; theory of the *gūṇas*, 38, 40-41
Sāṅkhya-Yoga; concept of atom, 47; time, 46; philosophy, 85
Sāṅkhya-Pātañjala, 83, 88
Science; *summum bonum* of Europe, 1; cultivation helped the development of Europe and America, 1; developed Hellenism, 2
Seal, B.N. (Dr.), 27, 64-65, 66, 88
Siddhāntaleśa, 13
(The) Smṛiti literature; growth, 51
Soul (*ātman*), 5; the Buddhist view, 56
(*The*) *Spandapradīpikā*; a treatise on Śaiva philosophy, 16
Sparśa, 68
Śṛidhara; concept of atom, 60; matter, 6
Śṛidhara-swamin, 78
Śriharṣa, 13
Śrimadbhāgavata, 75-76
Śrimadbhāgavat-gitā, 58
Śruti, 78
Stahl; phlogiston theory, 32-33
Substance; combination of atoms, 63
Super-infra-atomic theory of matter, 19
Suśruta, 64, 68; characterises *Kṣiti* and *Ap*, 67; classifications of animals, 76

(*The*) *Taittirīya Upaniṣad*; concept of five elements, 41
Tamas, 11
Tanmātras (infra-atomic potentials), 11; constitution, 67; genesis, 85-90
Tattvarthādhigama, 61
Tejas (light-heat substance), 13-14, 68, 69; characteristics, 66
Thing (*dravya*); *see* Qualities (*guṇas*)
Thing (*vastu*), 5
Thomson, J.J., 35
Time (*kāla*); concept of the Jainas, 45; Nyāya-Vaiśeṣika and Buddhist, 44; Sāṅkhya-Yoga, Vaiṣṇava and the grammar school, 44; *samaya*, *āvali*, *ucchvāsa*, *stoka*, *lava*, *ghati*, *muhūrtta*, day, 45
Transformation, 71
Trasareṇus, 9

Uddyotakara, 13; concept of atom, 60
Undifferentiated (*sāmyāvasthā*), 65
(The) Upaniṣad; characteristic, 53-55; *Chāndogya*, 38-40; doctrine of elements, 38, 43
Upaṣṭambhana, 62
Utpala, 16; concept of molecules, 59-60

Vācaspati, 13, 70-71, 72, 87, 88; concept of atom, 68; molecules, 60; velocity of *tejas*, 14
Vaiśeṣika, 28-29; 57; concept of atom, 42-43; elements, 43; evolution of matter, 43; matter, 6; motion, 24-25; Kaṇāda known as Pilupākavādins, 62
(The) Vaiṣṇava school; concept of *Prakṛiti* or *Māyā*, 18; did not accept atomic theory, 14; space, 44; time, 46; view of heaviness and lightness, 15
Vākyapadiya, 5, 16; concept of energy, 23-24
Vārttika, 13
Vasubandhu; Buddhist scholar, 6-7
Vāyu, 68; characteristics, 66
Vedānta, 13, 64, 88; concept of *Ākāśa*, 59; metaphysical side, 57; phenomenon of light, 19
(The) Vedic; sages speculation about the material objects, 40-41; view of life, 52-53
Velocity, 12
Veṅkaṭanātha Deśika; follower of

Rāmānuja, 10, 11, 15, 28-29, 41; conception of *gurutva*, 14-15; particles of matter, 47; space, 44
Vision, 32
Viṣṇupurāṇa; conception of plants and animals, 75, 78, 89
Vyāsa-bhāṣya, 58, 70, 71, 72, 85
World; external, 48; material, 57